CEO Guide to Doing Business in USA

By Ade Asefeso MCIPS MBA

Second Edition

ISBN-13: 978-1499580013

ISBN-10: 1499580010

Publisher: AA Global Sourcing Ltd
Website: http://www.aaglobalsourcing.com

Table of Contents

Disclaimer

This publication is designed to provide competent and reliable information regarding the subject matter covered. However, it is sold with the understanding that the author and publisher are not engaged in rendering professional advice. The authors and publishers specifically disclaim any liability that is incurred from the use or application of contents of this book.

Dedication

This book is dedicated to the hundreds of thousands of incredible souls in the world who have weathered through the up and down of recent recession.

To my family and friends who seems to have been sent here to teach me something about who I am supposed to be. They have nurtured me, challenged me, and even opposed me…. But at every juncture has taught me!

This book is dedicated to my lovely boys, Thomas, Michael and Karl. Teaching them to manage their finance will give them the lives they deserve. They have taught me more about life, presence, and energy management than anything I have done in my life.

Chapter 1: Why United State of America?

Are you a CEO, consultant, or entrepreneur interested in entering or expanding your business activity in the U.S. market?

Then this book is for you!

The main objective of this book is to provide you with basic knowledge about the USA; an overview of its economy, business culture, potential opportunities and an introduction to other relevant issues. Novice exporters, in particular will find it a useful starting point.

Some countries may be subject to export restrictions due to sanctions and embargoes placed on them by the UN or EU. Exporting companies are responsible for checking that their goods can be exported and that they are using the correct licences.

The USA has the largest and most technologically powerful economy in the world and is Britain's largest single export market.

There are four time zones across 50 states (Eastern, Central, Mountain and Pacific). The sheer size of the USA and vast cultural differences across the regions means that it should often be treated as a series of regional markets with varying characteristics. California alone, if considered as a separate country, would be the fifth largest country in the world based on its state gross product. New York, California, Texas, the

Midwest, and the South all have distinct cultures. In addition, there are further subdivisions within these regions making the U.S. market a fascinating and diverse place for UK exporters.

Opportunities in the USA

The U.S. economy is integrated and largely self-contained, with every major industry represented. U.S. manufacturers often source components overseas and UK goods have traditionally enjoyed a good reputation for quality in the United States.

Below are key sectors we identified in the United States:
- Advanced Engineering
- Clean Technology
- Creative and Media
- Energy and Power
- Financial and Professional Services
- Homeland Security
- ICT
- Life Sciences

Trade between UK and USA

The UK is the United States' fifth largest trading partner overall and second largest trading partner in the EU (in terms of goods). The USA is the UK's top export destination and second largest trading partner overall.

The UK is the largest foreign investor in the USA. At the end of 2008, UK had investment stock of $454 billion in the USA. Annual bilateral trade volume (in goods) increased steadily through 2008, reaching a record $112 billion that year

($58.6 billion from the UK to US, $53.8 billion from the US to the UK).

In 2008, the top four categories in which goods were traded between the US and UK were:

- Machinery and transportation equipment (imports from UK: $17.7 billion; exports to UK: $20.4 billion)
- Chemicals and pharmaceuticals (imports from the UK: $15.5 billion; exports to the UK: $7.7 billion)
- Miscellaneous manufactured articles (imports from UK: $6.6 billion; exports to UK: $9.5 billion)
- Mineral fuels, lubricants and related materials (imports from the UK: $8.5 billion; exports to the UK: $1.1 billion)

Chapter 2: Preparing to Export to the United State of America

The US economy is the largest national economy in the world. Freedom of the private sector, relatively low levels of regulation and government involvement, a productive and skilled labour force and high labour mobility have all been factors that have enabled the scale and growth of the US economy. GDP was estimated at $14.2 trillion in 2009 and economic growth has resumed since third quarter of 2009.

British citizens should note that all nationals and citizens of the UK are now required by law to obtain advance authorisation via the Electronic System for Travel Authorization (ESTA), prior to travelling to the United States under the Visa Waiver Program. The U.S. Government does not charge for ESTA registration. For more information see: https://esta.cbp.dhs.gov/esta

Visas

Travellers should make detailed enquiries about the appropriate visa and application procedures as far in advance of their intended visit as possible. For information on visa procedures and requirements in the USA, please visit the U.S. Embassy London web site at: http://london.usembassy.gov or contact the U.S. Embassy directly at:
U.S. Embassy London
24 Grosvenor Square
London
W1A 1AE
Tel: 020 7499 9000 (Switchboard)
Tel: 0904 245 0100 (Visa Contact Information)

http://www.aaglobalsourcing.com AA Global Sourcing Ltd's team in the USA can provide a range of services to British-based companies wishing to grow their business in the U.S. market. Our services include the provision of market information, validated lists of agents/potential partners, key market players or potential customers; establishing the interest of such contacts in working with the company; and arranging appointments. In addition, they can also organise events for you to meet contacts or promote a company and its products/services.

You can commission these services which are chargeable and operated by AA Global Sourcing Ltd to assist British-based companies wishing to enter or expand their business in overseas markets. Under this service, the teams; who have wide local experience and knowledge - can identify business partners and provide the support and advice most relevant to your company's specific needs in the market.

Chapter 3: Doing Business in United State of America

What companies should consider when doing business.

It is vital to do sufficient market research before attempting to export to the United States. The following is a non-exhaustive list of questions a company should consider before doing business in the USA.

1) What is the product? What does it do?

Sometimes the classification used for a product in the UK is different from that used in the USA. When doing initial research, be explicit about the product to ensure you receive the correct information.

2) Who are the end users?

It is important to understand who the ultimate end users of a product are. Otherwise, it will be difficult to identify the correct route to market.

3) How does the product reach the end users? (Who buys from me?)

Very few products in the U.S. market are sold directly to the end user. There is almost always a chain of importers, wholesalers, distributors, or some variation of that network. This chain of distribution impacts many factors including price, marketing, and packaging and is a key consideration for UK exporters.

4) How does my product compare to the competition?

It is important to learn about your competition before entering the US market. This effort will determine whether or not there is potential for your product or service, whether it can be sold profitably, and what features and benefits need to be emphasised or added.

5) Why should someone buy the product?

Differentiating a product from competitors is key. You should determine at an early stage which characteristics of your product you are going to emphasise. Cost is a favourite in the USA along with durability, unique features/benefits and after sales service.

6) What type of commission or remuneration do distributors, agents or representatives expect?

Each step in the chain of distribution will add a percentage to the original price of the product. The percentage varies by product and industry, but impacts the final cost to the end user. Just because your product is competitively priced to your primary customer (e.g. distributor, importer) does not mean the price to the end user will be as competitive.

Developing a realistic three to five year plan for sales is crucial. Both market size and competitive intelligence are essential elements to consider when developing a plan.

7) How will customer service be handled (warranties, returns, repairs?)

Customers in the USA expect a high level of customer service (e.g., an immediate response). E-mail, fax and telephone are the preferred method of communication.

Issues of warranties, returns, repairs and technical assistance must be handled in a manner equivalent to domestic competitors. UK telephone or fax numbers, manned only during UK business hours, will not be sufficient. Virtual office services can be arranged (e.g. toll free 1-800 numbers in the USA to ring through to the UK).

8) How much and how long can I afford to invest in the market before seeing a return?

It can take several years for a new company or product to be accepted in the USA and for significant sales to occur. UK companies must plan on this and consider the amount of time and money they are willing and able to invest.

9) Do I need an office in the USA?

Not necessarily, but you will need a U.S. point of contact and possibly a stockist of some nature, depending on your product.

If the product is small in size, an agent may often act as a stockist.

Products that are larger will require the use of contract warehouse facilities.

A U.S. office is not crucial if your sales efforts, address, customer issues and supply of spares can be effectively accomplished in another way. However, there are exceptions (e.g. the defence sector) where a local, U.S. office is nearly always necessary to secure contracts.

10) How do I find information on U.S. companies?

Information usually requested in the UK:
- Certification of Incorporation
- Directors' names and addresses
- Annual accounts and annual forms
- Full list of shareholder

U.S. equivalent to UK terms:
- Copy of the Articles of Incorporation & Amendments
- Copy of the Corporation's most recent completed Statement of Information, which is an annual statement filed with the Secretary of State. This lists the company's address, officers/directors, and agent for service of process and their addresses.
- Annual accounts and annual returns – though annual returns from the Franchise Tax Board is not public information.
- Shareholder information is NOT a public record in the USA. The majority of the states use their web presence to disseminate a range of public business records and most of them offer access at limited or no charge.

Gateways/Locations – Key areas for business

The capital city, political and administrative centre of the United States is Washington DC, but New York, Los Angeles and Chicago are all major industrial centres.

Other cities with populations over 0.5 million include: Atlanta, Boston, Buffalo, Cincinnati, Cleveland, Dallas, Denver, Detroit, Houston, Kansas City, Memphis, Miami, Milwaukee, Minneapolis, New Orleans, Phoenix, Pittsburgh, San Antonio, San Diego, San Francisco, San Jose, St Louis and Seattle.

The US Department of Labor Bureau of Labor Statistics web site (http://stats.bls.gov/) includes regional information, such as employment figures, by state.

Several state governments also have web sites containing local information. Some states have representation in Europe and form the Council of American States in Europe (CASE).

Chapter 4: Market Entry and Start up Considerations

When planning to establish a corporation or subsidiary in the USA it is essential to consult a lawyer familiar with both U.S. and UK regulation.

Potential Costs to Consider

1. Filing Fees for Incorporation. Expect these fees to vary from state to state.
2. Attorney's fees. Expect these fees to vary depending on the location and type of corporate entity.
3. Minimum Franchise Taxes. Some states within the USA impose substantial minimum franchise state taxes.
4. Office Space. Expect even shared office arrangements to be costly; more so for highly desirable locations.
5. Insurance. A business insurance package is necessary and can be costly.
6. One Employee Salary. Expect to pay the going rate for a basic salary, plus employment payroll taxes and employee benefits. These costs will be more in high cost-of-living cities like New York and San Francisco.
7. Immigration Visas. Visa fees costs thousands of dollars, and depend on several factors including location and choice of visa.

Customs and Regulations

All goods entering the USA are subject to duty on that their dutiable value unless specifically exempted by law. A good's dutiable value is determined in various ways and its duty varies according to its classification. Classification and valuation of the goods is the responsibility of the importer.

The U.S. Customs Service will then determine the relevant duty. Goods cannot leave the port of entry until the duty has been determined (liquidation). After liquidation importers have 90 days in which to appeal.

Depending on the product, a permit, licence or additional documentation may be required from other agencies such as FDA, (Food & Drug Administration) U.S. Fish and Wildlife, EPA (Environmental Protection Agency), or Department of Agriculture.

If you export or import into the USA, you need to know the Harmonized Tariff Schedule (HTS). This is a list of product codes for goods that are brought into the U.S., and the codes are linked to duty rates for specific products. Using the wrong code for a product can result in a company paying more duty than it should.

The Customs Classification Helpline can provide advice on tariff classification numbers. The Helpline is open from 08.30-17.00, and a voicemail service is available outside these hours. The contact telephone number is: +44 (0) 1702 366 077.

The United States International Trade Commission website www.dataweb.USITC.gov provides international trade statistics and U.S. Tariff data to the public full-time and free of charge.

Chapter 5: Legislation and Local Regulations

The Federal court system is based on English common law. Each state has its own unique legal system, of which all but one (Louisiana's) is based on English common law.

Responding to Tenders

FedBizOpps (www.fedbizopps.gov) is the government-wide point of entry for procurement opportunities. It has been designated as the single source for opportunities over $25,000, with 95 agencies and 21,296 contracting officers posting opportunities to the web site. It has a "proactive approach to federal sales and companies can quickly sign up to receive procurement information and sales opportunities."

The federal government can only contract with companies registered to do so. Central Contractor Registration (CCR) (www.ccr.gov/handbook.asp) is the central electronic registration site for companies wishing to be added to the U.S. federal government database of vendors.

Documentation

Imported goods generally require at a minimum the following documents:
- A bill of lading, airway bill or carrier's certificate
- A commercial invoice obtained from the seller that shows the value and description of the merchandise
- Entry manifest (Customs Form 7533) or Entry/Immediate Delivery (Customs Form 3461)

- Packing lists, if appropriate and other documents necessary to determine whether the merchandise may be admitted

The U.S. Customs and Border Protection web site www.cbp.gov provides very useful information on importing into the USA. Here you can access information on product labelling, country of origin markings and regulations.

Labelling and Packaging Regulations
All foods, drugs, medicines and cosmetics must have labelling or packaging that complies with the regulations of the Food and Drug Administration (FDA). All other products must comply with the regulations of the Federal Trade Commission (FTC).

Information regarding labelling and packaging requirements can be obtained by contacting the FTC; printed packaging and labelling requirements from the FDA; and general enquiries from the Consumer Product Safety Commission. Contact details for these organisations are listed below.

Federal Trade Commission
600 Pennsylvania Avenue,
NW Washington,
DC 20580
Tel: +1 202 326 2222
Web: www.ftc.gov

Food and Drug Administration
10903 New Hampshire Ave Silver Spring, Maryland 20993
Tel: +1 888 463 6332
Web: www.fda.gov

Chapter 6: Getting your Goods to the Market

As an exporter of goods you need to develop an understanding of various issues such as: legal and regulatory requirements your consignments have to comply with; paperwork involved; choosing the right mode of transport, i.e. road, air rail sea transport; protection for your goods; packaging; labelling; how freight forwarders can help you; rules for dangerous goods etc.

The British International Freight Association (BIFA) can provide assistance to companies who are new to exporting. There is a useful directory on the BIFA web site: (www.bifa.org). Choose "Search by detail" to select members by country, region or specialisation. A BIFA registered member can advise companies on such matters as modes of transport, distribution methods, costing, documentation and payment terms.

Standards and Technical Regulation

The American National Standards Institute (ANSI) provides accreditation in accordance with ISO/IEC Guide 65 for product certification programmes. You can make contact with their Customer Service Desk at:
American National Standards Institute
25 West 43rd Street
New York, NY 10036
Tele: +1 212 642 4980
Fax: +1 212 398 0023
Email: info@ansi.org

Web: www.ansi.org

Intellectual Property Rights

The Patent and Trademark Office (PTO) is an agency within the U.S. Department of Commerce. The ultimate 'goal' of the PTO is to orchestrate and grant patents for the protection of inventions and to register trademarks. The agency serves the needs and interests of both inventors and businesses with respect to their inventions and/or corporate products and their service identifications thereof. It also advises and assists various U.S. bureaux and other offices of the Department of Commerce and other agencies within the Government in matters involving 'intellectual property'.

U.S. Patent & Trademark Office
Mailstop USPTO Contact Centre
P.O. Box 1450
Alexandria, VA 22313 – 1450
Tel: +1 (571) 272 1000
Email: usptoinfo@uspto.gov
Web: www.uspto.gov

Business Etiquette

Citizens of the USA and the UK do not speak the same language!

Instructions, advertising copy and product descriptions that are acceptable in the UK may be not be understood in the USA. Literature and manuals produced in the UK are rarely acceptable in the U.S. market. U.S. standard size paper (8.5 inches by 11 inches) varies from A4 paper. Literature and manuals printed on A4 will not Xerox or fax properly and look odd in a group of U.S. standard sized papers. They should also be reviewed and amended to reflect American spelling and colloquialisms.

The U.S market largely revolves around networking: the way to tackle this market is to build relationships, attend events, and build your brand. Passive business styles do not work well; UK companies looking to enter this highly competitive market should be prepared to take a proactive approach.

Chapter 7: What are the Challenges?

The USA is an enormous market with huge potential and ostensibly a 'common language', but vast differences in geography and culture make it more like several markets. U.S. domestic companies approach their home market on a region by region basis for marketing, sales and distribution purposes. The size and variations in the market means that national representation is not standard; agents and distributors often work on a regional basis.

The USA is a very legalistic society. All contracts must be in writing and reviewed by legal counsel familiar with both UK and U.S. contractual law. All aspects of the agent/supplier relationship should be delineated, including obligations for financing of literature, travel and participation at trade events. Agent contracts in the USA customarily include agreed performance goals, termination, annual renewal, non-competitive clauses, and any authority to negotiate on behalf of the UK company.

Getting Paid - Terms of Payment

Terms of payment are various, but the following are some of the most commonly used:

Cash in advance: This is used by suppliers in the highest risk situations. Bear in mind that the supplier still has to determine when to officially accept the order from the U.S. firm. In other words, will goods be produced/ordered when the payment is received, or will the manufacturer produce/order the goods before hand and release the shipment upon receipt of advance payment? The later is obviously more risky.

Open account: The seller would need to specify a timeframe and the term would actually be noted as Net XX Days (usually 30). However, again the seller must bear in mind the following factors: 30 days from when? Date of invoice, bill of lading date, receipt of goods? All of this must be specified and absolutely clear to both parties in order to avoid loose interpretation on the part of the overseas customer. Overseas customers usually interpret 30 days as working days, which means the seller will most likely not receive payment for at least 45 days.

Sight Draft: This term requires bank involvement. There are numerous variations on the theme, but generally the seller; via his bank in some cases sends a type of cheque to the customer who, in essence, gives authority for that bank to draw funds in the amount specified in favour of the seller.

Letter of Credit (L/C): This is a very commonly used term in that it is the most secure form of payment. There are numerous variations, but a simple L/C is a secured draft that is passed between the buyer (opener) and seller (beneficiary) via intermediary banks which guarantee payment to variable extents.

The most commonly used type is a confirmed, irrevocable L/C which means that the L/C must involve a local bank friendly to the seller (confirmed) and that the buyer cannot back out of the arrangement (irrevocable).

L/Cs are very costly and depending on the cost of transaction can cost hundreds of dollars. An L/C payment term indicated on a proforma invoice could read something like this:

We will begin production upon receipt of indication that an irrevocable L/C has been opened in our favour and confirmed by a major London bank with all banking charges both inside and outside of the US for the account of buyer. As you can imagine, this form of payment takes a considerable amount of time and resources compared to the other terms of payment.

Chapter 8: How to Invest in the United State of America

In the United States, each state has its own Economic Development Office which can offer some specialised assistance including:

- Business climate, economy information, development news.
- Tax and financing help, enterprise zone information, business assistance and employee training programmes.
- Available buildings and sites, city & industry links.

Question you need to ask yourself before investing in the USA

1. Has your company been operating for more than two years and is it profitable?

2. Does your company export to or do business in any other international markets?

3. Do you have a web site and marketing materials that are appropriate for the US market?

4. Do you have sufficient time and resources to dedicate to US market entry?

5. Is there a market for your product/service in the USA or is the market already saturated?

6. Who and where are your potential customers and how do they currently purchase similar products?

7. How does your US or other competitors market their products?

8. Will the US customers require a US presence before taking your product seriously?

Chapter 9: Islamic Finance

Although the banking, insurance, wealth and asset management market in the USA is competitive, there are opportunities still to be found in other financial sectors. Islamic finance have only recently emerged as major markets in the USA and may be set up to see a more pronounced period of growth in the coming years.

Although Islamic Financing has had a presence in the USA for several years, many U.S. banks are only now fully realising the potential that this industry holds. This industry has truly picked up speed as more Pakistani and Middle-Eastern immigrants enter the USA. Pair that immigration surge along with a recent return to a stricter interpretation of the Quran for many Muslims, and we find that there is quite a large demographic of Muslims in the USA that are seeking out banks offering Shariah compliant loans.

This recent growth in demand has encouraged many of the largest banks in the world to have affiliates that are devoted to Islamic Finance.

Most of the Islamic Finance retail activity takes place in urban areas with large Muslim populations such as Chicago, Northern Virginia, Michigan, St. Paul/Minneapolis, Southern California and New York. Although there is some local community interest around Islamic finance in the USA, it still lags drastically behind Europe and the UK.

Experts say that there are still some regulatory and legal changes needed for Islamic finance to truly catch up in the USA, but the potential for this industry to grow remains.

The UK's objective in Islamic Finance is to communicate the attractiveness of the UK in this sector. A number of challenges remain to the development of Islamic Finance in the USA; these are:

- Finding trained personnel.
- The availability of adequate technology; it is relatively difficult to get customised software since the market is so small.
- Some observers believe that many institutions sell Shariah compliant products that do not meet the adequate standards of Islamic law.
- Islamic Finance is used as a marketing tool.
- New products have to be cleared in every state before they can be marketed.
- Public/Private Partnerships (PPP)

Chapter 10: Key Reasons to be Positive about the U.S. Market

The global infrastructure market in the USA is now showing concrete signs of developing into a significant opportunity for UK expertise. A combination of severe budget constraints, policy development, internal market pressure, increased understanding of the benefits of PPPs and recent lessons learnt, all combine to push real interest in the UK's long successful track record of PPP.

From its vast international experience, the UK can provide tailor-made solutions to suit the needs of widely varying economies across the world and specialised training courses for government officials who need to know how PPP really works.

U.S. infrastructure is in a generally poor state of repair - the American Society of Civil Engineers (ASCE) have estimated that some $2.2 trillion of investment in American infrastructure will be required over the next five years, at current levels of budgetary spend, there will be a massive $1.1 trillion shortfall. The highly publicised failure of the Interstate 35 bridge in Minnesota was only one of 160,570 U.S. bridges (out of a total of 590,750) that have been declared structurally deficient or functionally obsolete.

There is reportedly around $180 billion of private sector funds waiting on the sidelines, but earmarked for infrastructure investment.

Pension funds are increasingly viewing infrastructure as one of their core asset classes.

The recent American Recovery and Reinvestment Act (aka Stimulus Package) has a strong focus on infrastructure.

Only 27 cities have mass transit systems but 15 cities have plans for new systems to be built by 2030.

In addition to the above, the U.S. market is also beginning to broaden its outlook away from its current focus on PPP as a means to deliver transport infrastructure projects. Notable in this regard is the attempt by California to procure court houses through the P3 mechanism. Other key areas where the USA is likely to focus resources and will consider PPP models include:

- Mass transit
- Education
- Water.

Chapter 11: Business Services and Legal

The Business Services industry in the USA includes financial/management consulting firms, human resource & staff consulting firms, accounting companies, as well as law firms. The top consulting and law firms generally have offices located nationwide, and most have an international presence as well. There are a diverse number of firms ranging from small regional companies, to large international firms.

Business Service providers are facing a challenging time in the U.S. with new competitors and new demands from customers following the economic downturn.

Some of the challenges for UK companies targeting the U.S. Market include the following:

- The U.S Market is highly competitive, especially in the main financial hubs such as New York, Chicago and Los Angeles.
- UK companies will find it difficult to meet new clients if they don't understand the U.S. Market or have any market experience.
- It can be incredibly difficult to set up meetings with Fortune 500 companies, especially if the UK company has no unique offering.
- The skills required to negotiate successfully in the UK do not necessarily translate to success in the U.S. It is important for new companies to fully understand the U.S. Culture which can differ from State to State.

To overcome these challenges, UK service providers should simultaneously develop and deliver superior customer service while reducing costs and maximising the impact of every new investment.

Legal

There are plenty of opportunities in legal services because UK firms have the advantage of using Common Law which provides more certainty in areas such as dispute resolution and corporate liability. UK law firms also bring expertise in sectors where the UK is a world leader, such as Carbon Markets, PPP and Islamic Finance. Mid range UK law firms rely on referrals for a large proportion of their U.S. business. AA Global Sourcing Ltd, together with The Law Society, can help UK firms build a network of contacts with U.S. law firms. These contacts need to be diverse as U.S. law firms tend to be specialised by regions and by sectors.

Many of the top U.S. law firms are located in the New York, Washington, D.C. and Chicago areas, but there are also a vast number of medium to large sized firms located in cities all across the country. Priority regions for the promotion of UK legal services are those with the greatest trade in financial services, such as Los Angeles because of the concentration of high net worth individuals, Houston because of the large amount of Latin American business taking place in Texas, and Washington DC because of the presence of a number of high tech industries in North Carolina.

Chapter 12: Accounting and E-Finance

The change to International Financial Reporting Standards (IFRS) represented the most significant shift in financial reporting in the UK for more than a generation. Its implications reached far beyond technical accounting, and many companies found that their entire business practices had been impacted. UK accountants have extensive expertise in understanding the implications and processes of IFRS reporting. In this, they have an advantage over many U.S. firms and accountants.

The increasing acceptance of IFRS in the United States means that now is the time to become knowledgeable about these changes. In May 2010, the SEC held a meeting to discuss the current roadmap proposal to move to IFRS in the USA.

The SEC released a preliminary plan that would require US-listed companies to report under international accounting rules no earlier than 2015. UK accountants can look at this as an opportunity and become an invaluable resource for companies in the USA that are considering moving from UK GAAP to IFRS in the near future.

Financial technology firms have been impacted more than most sectors by the turmoil that has characterised the financial markets in the past months. As financial institutions, from banks to hedge funds, have come under growing scrutiny from bodies such as the SEC, technology providers have found themselves at the centre of increased vendor due diligence in the USA.

Interestingly, the demand for technology professionals on Wall Street is growing and has been since March 2010. Recruitment activity for technology professionals is up 24 percent year over year. The demand is coming from a wide array of financial services clients including bulge bracket banks, hedge funds, asset managers and consultants and vendors to the industry.

Which regions and cities are seeing the most demand? It's no surprise that New York City dominates given its status as the capital markets centre in the USA but we see demand in all the major market centres like Chicago, San Francisco, Boston and Philadelphia.

Due to banks facing stricter regulatory requirements, they are becoming more open to working with smaller, "best-in-class" providers that can provide greater flexibility than more established competitors. This shows that there are real opportunities for small and medium sized financial technology providers to sell solutions to the banking industry that would have previously been dominated by large global players.

The U.S. financial technology marketplace is characterised as dynamic and highly competitive but opportunities are there for firms who can differentiate themselves and stand out from the competition.

Chapter 13: Regional Analysis

Boston Consular District

The Boston Consular District covers all of New England including Eastern Connecticut, Rhode Island, Massachusetts, Vermont, New Hampshire, and Maine.

New England's financial services industry contributed $84 billion to the region's GSP in 2008, or 11 percent of the region's economic output making the industry the second largest sector by share of GSP in the region.

Massachusetts in particular is most active in asset management, asset servicing, insurance and private equity. Companies are able to draw from an extremely rich pool of highly educated workers with a history of innovation and a concentration of leading financial services companies. Massachusetts holds 15% of the global mutual fund asset management market and ranks third in the USA in terms of assets managed, trailing NY and California.

Massachusetts also ranks second for venture capital, after California with over 250 venture capital and private equity firms with offices in Massachusetts and Boston ranks third in per-capita private equity spending. While Boston remains a favoured location for many front office jobs, Rhode Island and New Hampshire have been creating low-cost, low-tax attractive environments for middle and back-office functions.

Chicago Consular District

The Chicago consular district covers the Midwestern United States, which is a geographic area larger than the whole of Western Europe. The region accounts for 22 percent of U.S. GDP, and is made up of the following fourteen states: Colorado, Illinois, Indiana, Iowa, Kansas, Kentucky, Michigan, Minnesota, Missouri, Nebraska, North Dakota, Ohio, South Dakota and Wisconsin.

The Midwest is home to the headquarters of 149 of the Fortune 500 companies, including many leading financial services businesses. The region represents a broad base of economic activity and most financial service sub-sectors are well represented.

Chicago is the United States' second largest financial and business services centre and the eighth largest financial services market in the world. The Chicago Mercantile Exchange is the world's largest derivatives exchange and Des Moines, Iowa, has the second largest concentration of captive insurers in the United States.

Houston Consular District

The Houston Consular District covers Texas, Arkansas, Colorado, Louisiana, Oklahoma and New Mexico. As the energy capital of the USA, Houston's financial services industry is strongly influenced by the needs of the energy sector. As a result, most of the world's major investment banks have an office in Houston where mergers and acquisitions activity in the North American oil & gas industry takes place.

Additionally, Texas-based boutique investment banks also service the energy industry. Dallas and Houston are home to large private equity firms, including Texas Pacific Group, as well as energy hedge funds, and over-the-counter derivatives trading firms.

Dallas also has a strong presence in asset management and features some of the largest financial institutions in the state. However, the majority of Texas' 327 state's chartered banks, which hold $164.7 billion in assets, are mostly small regional banks. Texas also boasts an active venture capital and angel investor community.

Important themes for the future include carbon finance, as Houston aims to become the Carbon Trading Capital of the USA, as well as Legal, Software and Islamic Finance, which have yet to see their full potential in the region.

New York Consular District

The New York Consular District covers four states including New York, Connecticut, New Jersey, and Pennsylvania. As the preeminent global financial centre in the USA, many of the country's leading investment banks, asset management companies, securities brokers and insurance firms continue to call this region home. In addition, many leading foreign finance and business services firms have their North American headquarters located in this region.

New York sources a large volume of its business from its domestic market and dominates in sectors such as fund management, hedge fund assets, private equity and securitisation. In recent years Connecticut has grown as a hotspot for finance along with New York, as many top hedge funds have settled down in towns like Greenwich and Stamford.

Additionally, nine of the top twenty largest law firms in the nation are headquartered in either New York or Philadelphia. Industry sectors that have yet to reach their full potential in the New York Consular District include Islamic Financing, Carbon Financing and Public-Private Partnerships. These industries are poised to expand and grow in the coming years.

Los Angeles Consular District

The Los Angeles Consular District includes Southern California, Utah, Nevada (Clark County), Hawaii and Arizona. Los Angeles is the second largest city in the United States, with a population of 4 million.

The banking and finance industry in Los Angeles is one of the largest in the United States. More than 100 foreign and countless domestic banks operate branches in Los Angeles, along with many financial law firms and investment banks. UAFS (Utah Association of Financial Services) organisations, which include industrial banks, savings banks, and non depository finance companies have grown to more than $241 billion dollars in assets and is one of Utah's largest business sectors. Arizona is geographically the sixth largest state in the Union with an area of 113,956 square miles.

Miami Consular District

Miami covers Florida, Georgia, Tennessee, Puerto Rico and the U.S. Virgin Islands. Most of the financial service activity in the region is concentrated in Miami, Florida and Atlanta, Georgia. Florida is home to nearly 123,000 financial and related professional service establishments that employ approximately 900,000 people. The area also has a developing wealth management competency.

Over 70 foreign and domestic banks have offices in Florida, including six of the ten largest in the world. Additionally, Miami is home to a growing number of international law firms such as Greenberg Traurig LLP and Diaz Reus & Targ, LLC.

Atlanta has the nation's third largest concentration of Fortune 500 companies and the world's busiest airport. The city has a sizeable financial services sector with more than ten international banks in the area, and is a growing hub for e-finance activity.

Additionally, Atlanta is home to a large number of international law firms. Public-private-partnerships (PPP) is an industry sector poised to expand dramatically in the coming years.

In 2009 Florida was home to two of only three PPP projects in the United States. Additionally both Georgia and Puerto Rico have opened a large number of projects for international PPP activity.

San Francisco Consular District

The San Francisco Consular District includes Northern California, Northern Nevada, Oregon, Washington, Idaho, Wyoming and Alaska. The San Francisco Bay Area is the leading financial centre within the San Francisco Consular District.

The Bay Area is a $200 billion annual economy ranking 21st in the world. Twenty-six Fortune 500 companies are headquartered in California, which ranks second only to New York. The San Francisco Bay Area financial services sector is concentrated in venture capital and private equity and has the highest density of venture capital firms in the world.

The leading venture capital firms based in the Bay Area include Kleiner Perkins Caulfield & Byers, Sequoia Capital, New Enterprise Associates and Draper Fisher Jurvetson. In 2008, the Bay Area saw the most venture capital deals compared to all other U.S. cities, with $11 billion in investments and 1,207 deals closed. The San Francisco Bay Area is a vibrant, entrepreneurial place which supports innovation across all sectors, including financial services.

Washington D.C. Consular District

The Washington DC Consular District includes Delaware, Maryland, Virginia, West Virginia as well as North and South Carolina. The largest employer in the Washington, DC area is of course the federal government. Law and Lobby firms are high on the list of affluent businesses in the DC area with over 800 law practices covering Litigation, Business & Corporate Law, Intellectual Property, Criminal Law and more.

Within this Consular Region, 44 companies are listed in the Fortune 500, with North Carolina hosting the most Financial Services companies such as Bank of America, BB&T and Wachovia.

Delaware has partnered with many innovative and dynamic financial companies around the globe, thereby establishing the State as the place for international financial institutions looking to enter U.S. markets. Delaware's pro-business legal and regulatory environment, strategic positioning, and landmark legislation, such as the Financial Centre Development Act, have paved the way for the financial services industry to become a key component of Delaware's economic strength and growth.

This cluster comprised of a large, interconnected community of credit card banks, commercial banks, non-banking financial entities, investment advisors, insurance companies, trust entities, and service providers.

Chapter 14: United Kingdom Opportunities in the United State of America

The United States is a relatively open global economy and has a history of supporting liberalization in overseas trade and investments. Apart from a few import quotas and strategic industry-ownership restrictions, British firms doing business in the USA face few barriers.

It is Britain's largest single export market, taking £28.5 billion of UK goods in 2004. The UK is sixth biggest exporter to the US, after Canada, Mexico, China, Japan and Germany. The US is also the leading overseas destination for British investment.

There are, and over the short to medium term will be, significant opportunities for exporting and/or direct investment in the Environmental Goods and Services (EGS) markets of solid waste management, water utilities and wastewater treatment, air pollution abatement and in the Carbon Abatement Technologies (CATs) markets with regard to fossil fuels and renewable energy.

The US market for EGS was estimated at US$241 billion in 2004. This represented a 5% growth on the 2003 figure of US$229 billion and comprised about 38% of the 2004 global environmental market. The largest segment in terms of both revenue and employment is solid waste management (US$26 billion and 206,000 employees).

The most recent Environmental Protection Agency drinking water survey (2003 data) found that the country's water systems will need to invest an estimated US$277 billion between 2003 and 2023. Large investments are also expected in landfill capacity within solid waste management as landfill sites continue to decline and waste increases. The US water/wastewater industry is expected to require significant spending in infrastructure in the coming years.

A relatively large and growing market that typically falls into the clean technology category is the green building industry. A recent Frost and Sullivan report estimated the US green building industry revenues of US$12 billion in 2007, and this figure could rise to approximately US$42 billion by 2015.

A patchwork of environmental regulations and policies has been in operation across the US for some time. As a member of the UNFCC, it is increasing pressure to monitor and reduce CO_2 emissions. The US Clean Air Act has been a historical driver of domestic demand. State governments have made clean energy, energy efficiency and climate change initiatives high priorities. Almost every state has enacted GHG emissions inventories and many have state-led clean energy programs. California has the most stringent regulations, being the only state with a state-wide GHG emissions cap.

Other drivers of EGS and CATs markets in the US are economic; the number of landfill sites is set to decline while waste continues to increase. The US is a huge consumer of energy and current predictions forecast even greater demands over the next 20 years.

Almost half the electricity generated in the US is from coal and US coal-fired plants have over 300 GW of capacity. Of these, approximately one-third date from 1970 or earlier, the most of the rest from 1970-1989. Only 12 coal-fired plans have been built since 1990.

The country's growing appetite for energy, coupled with a rising environmental awareness and a push towards policies for combating environmental damage while achieving energy security suggests that the market for environmental goods and services and carbon abatement technologies should continue to expand.

There is a growing demand from America's largest companies for EGS, particularly waste reduction. For example, Wal-Mart illustrates the increasing awareness that US "big business" can achieve efficiencies and cost reductions through applying EGS.

Initiatives aimed at stimulating the deployment of renewable energy technologies have numerous drivers in the US. Primarily, there is concern to address the growing energy demand, but other influences play a role, such as, reducing the adverse effects on the environment, encouraging the economic development of domestic industries, and providing reliable, diversified energy sources.

The largest renewable energy sources are hydroelectric (42%), woody biomass (31%), and biofuels (11%). The US Government is backing the production of biofuels. They are seen as a way to stimulate US domestic farm revenues, increase the US energy security, and help reduce the negative environmental effects of fossil fuel consumption.

Chapter 15: Overview of United State of America Water Sector

The broadly defined US water sector represented approximately US$124 billion in revenues in 2008, growing 4-5% over 2007 figures. Water utilities (about 70% public sector) and wastewater treatment works (more than 95% public sector) each account for about one-third of these annual revenues, with various equipment and services accounting for the rest. The Instruments and Analytical Service sub-sector accounted for approximately one percent of these revenues.

In general, business conditions are satisfactory for US water sector participants, but there is clear concern for the impacts of the economy on the spending ability of their predominantly municipal, regional and federal funded or at least federally driven customer base. The consensus among industry insiders is that there will be a fairly notable drop-off in growth rates, according to the more than 70 firm leaders who responded to Environmental Business Journal's Water & Wastewater Market & Opinion Survey 2008.

The US commercial water and wastewater utilities industry includes about 5,000 companies with combined revenues of US$9 billion. Large companies include American Water Works, Aqua America, California Water Service and the US subsidiaries of major global player, including United Water (a subsidiary of SUEZ Environnement) and Veolia Water North America (subsidiary of Veolia Environnement).

The industry is fairly concentrated; the 50 largest companies account for about 65% of the industry revenue. The commercial industry is small compared to the water and wastewater services operated by many regional and local governments in the US.

Competitive Landscape

Demand depends on commercial and residential water needs, which are related to population growth and to the level of economic activity. The profitability of individual companies depends on efficiency of operations, because prices are fixed by public utility commissions (PUCs).

Large companies have economies of scale in operations and the ability to raise capital for infrastructure improvements. Small companies can compete successfully through superior engineering or by serving smaller, local markets.

High barriers to entry, such as capital investments, can make the industry somewhat resistant to competition and many companies operate as de facto monopolies.

Issues that affect water supply and sanitation in the US include water scarcity, pollution, a backlog of investment, concerns about the affordability of water for the poorest, and a rapidly retiring workforce.

Increased variability and intensity of rainfall as a result of climate change is expected to produce both more severe droughts and flooding, with potentially serious consequences for water supply and for pollution from combined sewer overflows. Droughts are likely to particularly affect the 66 percent of Americans whose communities depend on surface water. As for drinking water quality, there are concerns about disinfection by-products, lead, perchlorates and pharmaceutical substances, but generally, drinking water quality in the US is good.

Cities, utilities, state governments and the federal government have addressed these issues in various ways. To keep pace with demand from an increasing population, utilities traditionally have augmented supplies. However, faced with increasing costs and droughts, water conservation is beginning to receive more attention and is being supported through the federal Water Sense program. The reuse of treated wastewater for non-potable uses is also becoming increasingly common. Pollution through wastewater discharges, a major issue in the 1960s, has been brought largely under control.

Water supply and wastewater systems are regulated by state governments and the federal government. At the state level, health and environmental regulation is entrusted to the corresponding state-level departments. Public Utilities Commissions or Public Service Commission's regulate tariffs charged by private utilities.

In some states they also regulate tariffs by public utilities. At the federal level, drinking water quality and wastewater discharges are regulated by the US Environmental Protection Agency, which also provides funding to utilities through State Revolving Funds.

Most Americans are served by publicly owned water and sewer utilities. Eleven percent of Americans receive water from private (so-called "investor-owned") utilities. In rural areas, cooperatives often provide drinking water.

Finally, up to 15% of Americans are served by their own wells. Water consumption in the US is more than double that in Central Europe, with large variations between the states. In 2002, the average American family spent $474 on water and sewerage charges, which is about the same level as in Europe.

Chapter 16: Infrastructure and Water Use

The centralized drinking water supply infrastructure in the US consists of dams and reservoirs, well fields, pumping stations, aqueducts for the transportation of large quantities of water over long distances, water treatment plants, reservoirs in the distribution system (including water towers), and nearly 2 million miles of distribution lines. Depending on the location and quality of the water source, all or some of these elements may be present in a particular water supply system. In addition to this infrastructure for centralized network distribution, about 15% of Americans rely on their own water sources, usually wells.

About 90% of public water systems in the US obtain their water from groundwater. However since systems served by groundwater tend to be much smaller than systems served by surface water, only about 35% of Americans (101 million) are supplied with treated groundwater, while 65% (195 million) are supplied with surface water. For a surface water system to operate without filtration, it has to fulfill certain criteria set by the US EPA under its Surface Water Treatment Rule, including implementation of a watershed control program. For example, the water system of New York City has repeatedly fulfilled these criteria.

The centralized sanitation infrastructure in the US consists of more than 1.2 million miles of sewers, including both sanitary sewers and combined sewers - sewage pumping stations and over 16,000 publicly-owned wastewater treatment plants. In addition, at least 17% of Americans are served by on-site sanitation such as septic tanks. Publicly owned wastewater treatment plants serve approximately 190 million people and treat more than 32 billion gallons per day, approximately 9,400 facilities provide secondary treatment, 4,430 facilities provide advanced treatment, and 2,030 facilities do not discharge.

There are approximately 175 facilities that provide a treatment level that is less than secondary. These include facilities with ocean discharge waivers, and treatment facilities discharging to other facilities meeting secondary treatment or better.

Water Use

Public water supply used 43 billion gallons per day in 2000 serving 242 million people, corresponding to 21% of total water use in the same year. Residential (home) water use accounts for 66% of publicly supplied water in the US, with the remainder being used by offices, public buildings, businesses and industry that does not have its own water sources. Residential end use of water in the US is equivalent to more than 1 billion glasses of tap water per day. Total water use was 161 gallons per capita per day in 1996-1998 excluding leakage. Approximately 60% is used outdoors for gardening, swimming pools, etc. corresponding to 101 gallons per capita per day, and 42% is used indoors, corresponding to 60 gallons. The arid West has some of the highest per capita residential water use because of landscape irrigation.

Per capita residential water use in the US is more than four times as high as in the UK and five times as high as in Germany. Only a small share of public water supply is used for drinking. According to one 2002 survey of 1000 households, an estimated 56% of Americans drank water straight from the tap and an additional 37% drank tap water after filtering it. Approximately 75% of Americans said they bought bottled water.

Chapter 17: United State of America Water Service Providers

Currently there are approximately 54,000 community public water systems in the US, which are either publicly owned cooperatives or privately owned, serving a total of about 309 million in September 2010. Approximately 4,000 systems provide water in localities with more than 10,000 inhabitants, and the remaining 50,000 systems provide water in localities with less than 10,000 inhabitants. In 2010, 15% of Americans (45 million people) relied on their own water source, usually a well for drinking water.

Utilities in charge of public water supply and sanitation systems can be owned, financed, operated and maintained by a public entity, private company or both can share responsibilities through a public-private partnership. Utilities can either be in charge of only water supply and/or sanitation, or they can be in charge of providing other services, in particular, electricity and gas. In the latter case, they are called multi-utilities.

Bulk water suppliers are entities that manage large aqueducts and sell either treated or untreated water to various users including utilities. Approximately 90% of Americans served by a public water system are served by a public or cooperative entity. Usually public systems are managed by utilities that are owned by a city or county, but have a separate legal personality, management and finances.

About half of American drinking water utilities, or about 27,000, are privately owned, providing water to 11% of Americans served by public water systems. Most of the private utilities are small but a few are large and are traded on the stock exchange. The largest private water company in the US is American Water, which serves approximately 15 million customers in 1,600 communities in the US and Canada. It is followed by United Water, which serves 7 million customers and is owned by the French firm, Suez Environnement.

Overall, about 34 million Americans get water from a privately owned drinking water utility. In addition, 20% of all wastewater utilities in the US are privately owned many of them relatively small. In addition, more than 1,300 government entities (typically municipalities) contract with private companies to provide water and /or wastewater services.

Some utilities in the US provide only water and/or sewer services, while others are multi-utilities that also provide power and gas services. There are also a few large bulk water suppliers in the arid Southwest US, which sell water to utilities.

Chapter 18: Water and Sanitation Service Provider Regulation

The economic regulation of water and sanitation service providers in the US (particularly in relation to the setting of user water rates) is usually the responsibility of regulators such as Public Utility Commissioners at the state level. While all investor-owned utilities are subject to tariff regulation only a few public utilities are subjected to the same regulation. In fact, only 12 states have laws restricting pricing practices by public water and sanitation utilities.

The environmental and drinking water quality regulation is the responsibility of state departments of health or environment and the US EPA. National Primary Drinking Water Regulations (NPDWRs or primary standards) are legally enforceable standards that apply to public water systems. Primary standards protect public health by limiting the levels of contaminants in drinking water.

The Safe Drinking Water Act (SDWA) is the principal federal law concerning drinking water. SDWA authorized the US EPA to promulgate regulations regarding water supply. The major parts are found in the Code of Federal Regulations. Parts 141, 142 and 143 regulate primary contaminants, implementation by states and secondary contaminants. Primary contaminants are those with health impacts.

State implementation allows states to be the primary regulators of the water supplies (rather than the EPA) provided they meet certain requirements. Secondary contaminants generally cause aesthetic problems and are not directly harmful. The SDWA also contains provisions that require water suppliers to develop emergency plans, water supply operators to be licensed and watersheds to be protected.

Chapter 19: Opportunities in Water Monitoring and Instrumentation

The ability to monitor, track and understand the implications of the physical and chemical composition of water is becoming increasingly critical. As a more informed public demands better information about its drinking water, as new and more comprehensive regulatory controls evolve, and as new contaminant effects are better understood, testing and monitoring requirements are sure to grow.

This sector of the water business consists of numerous different components, including suppliers of fixed-base analytical laboratory equipment, in-line and field water-quality measurement devices, data analysis systems, water meters and various quantity measurement devices, data analysis systems, collection and transmission systems, and analytical software packages as well as providers of commercial testing and analysis services. Taken together, industry experts estimate that the water monitoring and testing business represents annual revenue of approximately $5 billion per year and is widely agreed that this area will be one of the most rapidly growing sectors within the water industry.

There have been a number of developments over the past decade that have thrust the monitoring and testing business into the critical centre of the water industry. First and foremost, since the original passage of the Clean Water Act in the early 1960s, there has been a gradually increasing level of public concern about water resources and water quality, and continuing thirst for better understanding of the impact of water quality on human health.

This growing public concern has gradually translated into broader and more extensive water-quality regulation in the US and around the world. Today, most developed countries have comprehensive water pollution control regulations and compliance requirements, which require extensive testing and monitoring of water at each step of the treatment and distribution process. A key development is the dramatic advance in analytical technology. New capabilities now allow detection of chemicals in water at extremely low levels of concentration parts per billion or even parts per trillion.

This improving ability to identify ultra-low-level contaminants has led to a new level of concern about water quality. In many cases, there is little understanding of the potential impact, if any, of these newly identified contaminants and compounds. As the public becomes aware of ultra-low-level contaminants in drinking water supplies, a new round of concern and additional testing requirements will probably result.

As part of the response to these trends, advanced real-time monitoring processes and dependable remote and field deployable instruments and monitors have begun to be used on a wide scale. In the past, a manufacturer only knew it had water quality problems when it began to produce off-spec product; the water utility knew it had problems after the local emergency room began to fill up.

Today, both industry and utilities monitor in-coming source waters and treated discharge waters on a much more real-time basis, so that they can anticipate issues or problems rather than simply react to them after the fact.

Changes affecting the water quality monitoring and testing market are also occurring on the industrial side of the business. Industrial processes that require ultrapure have perhaps the most demanding monitoring and testing requirements. For example, in the pharmaceutical and semiconductor industries, analytical devices can represent a significant portion of the capital costs of water treatment.

Very sensitive devices with fast response times are required for analyzing ultra-low-level potential contaminants. Increasing public awareness and better understanding of the impact of varying water quality will continuously translate into broader regulatory requirements. The increasing frequency of water shortages globally and growing concerns about water security imply greater demand for secure management and control systems, and the requisite data and analysis. Because the water industry is suffering from a growing shortage of qualified personnel, all forms for automation in water monitoring and testing will be a growing focus, to enable greater efficiency and productivity.

Chapter 20: Sales Channels to the U.S. Market

Companies supplying customers in the United States often choose to sell their products and services either directly to the customer or through sales representatives, distributors, or franchisees. The applicable legal rules may vary depending upon the precise nature of the legal relationship between the parties.

1. Direct Sales

Selling goods directly to customers in the United States creates a bilateral contractual relationship between the non-US seller and the US purchaser. On their face, contracts for sale in the United States and many other foreign countries all involve a common concept, the delivery of goods in exchange for payment of money.

There are, however, distinct differences between the common law jurisdiction of the United States and civil law jurisdictions (e.g., Continental European jurisdictions). Although US law in this regard may differ from state to state, the sale provisions of the United States generally are based on Article 2 of the Uniform Commercial Code, or UCC. In many respects, these US rules fundamentally diverge from the rules of European civil law, for example, which are based on Roman law principles:

1. Under the laws of certain civil law jurisdictions, an offer has a binding effect for the time it is held open by the offeror or, in the absence of a fixed period of time, for a time of reasonable duration. Under US law an offer (apart from a so-called "firm offer") is in

principle revocable as long as the acceptance has not yet been dispatched by the offeree.

2. Under the laws of certain civil law jurisdictions, the party suffering from the breach of contractual duties by the other party has the right to claim "performance in kind," as long as such performance is feasible, whereas a decree for specific performance is available in the United States under the UCC only with regard to "unique goods" and in "proper circumstances".

3. Under the laws of certain civil law jurisdictions, a merchant buyer has the duty to inspect a purchased good immediately after delivery and, if it proves to be defective, to give notice of the defect without further delay. The duty is strict and if the merchant fails to protest in as short a time as possible, bearing in mind the circumstances of the case, then the buyer loses all remedies against the seller. In the United States, similar strict time provisions do not apply and the consequences for failure to observe such rules are less severe; and

4. Under the laws of certain civil law jurisdictions, one of the remedial consequences to a minor defect of a purchased good is a claim for "reduction in price," which differs from a claim for damages under the US system, among other ways, due to the timing and method for calculating the monetary compensation for defective performance.

Several other differences abound and the above list is intended to illustrate only a few examples and demonstrate that legal advice should be sought by non-US companies when drafting a contract (including standard terms and conditions of sale) for sales in the United States.

2. Sales Representatives, Distributors and Franchisees

A sales representative is appointed to contact potential customers and solicit (but, normally, not accept) orders for goods or services. A sales representative, sometimes called a sales agent, generally is compensated by receiving a commission from the manufacturer. There are few US legal limitations upon appointing sales representatives, and the principal generally may impose territorial, price and other restrictions.

Most states do not have specific termination protection laws (in terms of mandatory notice periods or compensation), although principals are under an obligation to deal in good faith with their representatives.

In contrast, a distributor typically buys a manufacturer's products for resale, earning a profit via the mark-up charged on the goods sold. Accordingly, the distributor is usually considered to be an independent contractor who bears the economic risk of the sales transaction. Thus, absent extenuating circumstances, a manufacturer will not be held liable for the acts and promises of the distributor.

US antitrust laws limit the ability of a foreign company to impose territorial, price or other restrictions upon a distributor. However, most states do not grant distributors any special rights or compensation upon termination.

Finally, a franchisee in the United States involves more than a simple product distribution arrangement. Franchises are not limited to fast-food and retail establishments, but can cover many products and services. Many franchise arrangements include a fully-integrated relationship with the parent company involving marketing strategies, control of operational methods, up-front franchise fees, quality controls and communication systems.

A detailed discussion of US franchising law is beyond the scope of this book, but certain general observations can be made. Franchise relationships are governed by both federal and state law. The Federal Trade Commission, or FTC, regulates franchising at the federal level.

While the FTC does not directly regulate franchise terms or impose any registration requirements, it does require franchisors to disclose certain information to prospective franchisees. Generally, however, states regulate franchising more extensively than the federal government.

Individual states may require:
- Registration of franchises prior to their offer or sale;
- Mandatory disclosure of certain information, delivered to prospective franchisees within certain periods of time before sale;
- Regulation of the advertising for the sale of franchises, terminations of, and refusals to renew franchises, and the registration of franchise sales persons; and
- Regulations regarding misrepresentations and other unfair practices.

Chapter 21: General Terms and Conditions

Foreign companies doing business in the United States should be cognizant of the fact that the terms and conditions to which they are accustomed or that are set forth in their documentation may not ultimately govern under US law. Moreover, even if they do govern, such foreign-oriented terms may not be sufficient to address the issues and pitfalls that typically arise under commercial agreements and arrangements in the United States.

When purchase documentation of a buyer directly contradicts the sale documentation of a seller, for example, a situation referred to as the "battle of the forms" results. To the extent such disputes are ever litigated in the United States, foreign companies are frequently disappointed with the outcome.

Likewise, foreign companies that are inclined to rely on the documentation of their US counterpart (customer or supplier) to memorialize the business relationship need to understand that such documentation, as a matter of practice, is very favourable to the drafting party, and in the event of a dispute will almost always work to the advantage of their US counterpart. Simply translating or attempting to "Americanize" a non-US company's standard form will in most cases be insufficient to address issues that may arise in the United States.

Instead, such companies are best served by preparing a US standard purchase or sales form on the basis of which they may negotiate and define in writing the applicable terms and conditions of the respective purchase/sale arrangement.

Warranties

A foreign company selling goods in the United States should also be aware of certain warranties that accompany the sale of goods and provide to a buyer certain legal remedies if breached. Article 2 of the UCC governs warranties arising in connection with the sale of goods.

There are two types of warranties under the UCC: express warranties and implied warranties. An express warranty is created by any promise or affirmation of fact made by the seller. If the seller states expressly that the goods sold have certain qualities, but they do not, the buyer could sue the seller for breach of warranty.

But even if the seller remains silent as to certain qualities of a product, the seller under US law is still deemed to have made certain implied promises by merely selling the product. An example of an implied warranty is the implied warranty of merchantability by selling certain goods, a seller under US law represents that the goods are of a quality normally acceptable in the particular trade and fit for their ordinary purpose.

In the event that goods fail to conform to this warranty, the buyer, as in all other cases of breach of warranty, is entitled to recover damages (which can include incidental or consequential damages) incurred by the buyer as a result of the breach.

Chapter 22: Secured Transactions

Another critical and idiosyncratic issue in connection with selling goods in the United States is the law of secured transactions. Unlike some European jurisdictions, for example, US law does not provide for the legal concept of a so-called "retention of title." Generally, a seller in the United States does not retain legal title in the goods sold until receipt of the full purchase price. Instead, under US law, after executing the purchase agreement, legal title passes over to the buyer.

Sellers in the United States protect their interest in goods sold (but not yet paid in full) by obtaining a so-called "security interest." The law of security interests in the United States is established by Article 9 of the UCC. A detailed discussion of the innumerable nuances of Article 9 of the UCC is beyond the scope of this book. However, a review of fundamental concepts may be appropriate and helpful.

Two key concepts applicable to the creation and operation of security interests under Article 9 of the UCC are "attachment" and "perfection." Attachment is the term of art describing when a security interest is said to exist between a creditor (the seller of the goods) and a debtor (the buyer of the goods). In order for a security interest to attach to a debtor's collateral, five steps are typically required:

1. The creditor must give value, usually by advancing money or other funds, to the debtor;
2. The debtor must have rights in the collateral;
3. There must be a security agreement;
4. The security agreement must describe the collateral; and

5. Either the security agreement must be in a writing signed by the debtor or there must be some other "authenticating" event to prove that the parties have entered into a security agreement.

While a security interest must first be found to have attached to the collateral, often the true value of the security interest is the priority it grants the secured lender over certain classes of other creditors. The relationship between the secured lender and other third-party creditors is governed mainly by "perfection." Because a perfected secured creditor is typically granted priority over other, non-perfected creditors claiming an interest in the collateral, having a properly "perfected" security interest is critical to any secured creditor.

Perfection can be accomplished through numerous methods, including the creditor taking possession of the collateral, and may even, in certain circumstances, occur automatically. However, the most common method for a secured lender to perfect a security interest is by filing a financing statement.

A financing statement is a public document which at a minimum: declares the identity of the creditor and the debtor; describes the collateral; provides a mailing address for the debtor and creditor; and answers if the debtor is an organization or an individual. Additionally, the filing must be properly communicated and the filing fee must be tendered.

Finally, if the collateral is real estate, other restrictions may apply. In all "perfection" situations, the filing requirements need to be reviewed and adhered to carefully.

Another creditor-friendly aspect of perfection can be illustrated by the following hypothetical.

Assume, for example, that the holder of a security interest is a British manufacturer selling a piece of machinery into the United States through a US distributor. What if a US customer buys the piece of machinery from the US distributor and seeks to maintain priority over the British manufacturer's security interest in the piece of machinery?

Generally, if certain additional requirements are fulfilled, a third party buying goods in the good faith belief that a seller had the capacity to validly transfer legal title will in fact, by operation of law, acquire legal title in these goods. The British manufacturer will not be left behind with empty hands, however. If it had a perfected security interest in the piece of machinery, the security interest will, in most cases, automatically perfect in the proceeds of the sale, i.e., in a cheque or cash, giving the manufacturer a potent tool to go after the distributor for the proceeds of the sale.

From a manufacturer's perspective, the procedures of attaching and perfecting a security interest probably appear to be cumbersome. Article 9 of the UCC, in accordance with the general ethos of the UCC to provide and accommodate commercial realities, does not aim at inhibiting the free flow of trade. Thus, Article 9 allows a manufacturer selling its goods in the United States to obtain a purchase money security interest, or PMSI, in the machinery that it sells to a distributor on credit. The manufacturer will hold the PMSI until the distributor pays the purchase price. The PMSI is relatively easy to obtain: if properly attached, a PMSI is perfected automatically by operation of law, sparing the manufacturer from, as the case may be, having to file a financing statement. In addition, the PMSI takes precedence over certain other perfected secured interests of third party creditors, such as banks, making it somewhat of a super-security interest.

In summary, a foreign company selling goods in the United States must be mindful of the intricacies of secured transactions. Article 9 of the UCC is a detailed provision and contains numerous pitfalls. It is relatively easy for a security interest to be improperly attached or perfected, leaving a seller without any priority recourse against a defaulting buyer.

Chapter 23: Key Business-Related Aspects of Doing in United State of America

This chapter describes several key business-related aspects of doing business in US.

Product Liability

Extensive laws regarding product liability and compensation for damages sustained by users of products exist in the United States. Similar to other countries, manufacturers that sell in the United States are liable for any damages sustained as a result of negligence on behalf of the manufacturer (or seller). Additionally, liability may occur for any breach of warranty.

Certain manufacturers and sellers may be held strictly liable for damages caused by their products under certain conditions. Most companies selling in the United States obtain product liability insurance, either in the United States or in their home countries.

Unfair Trade

The Federal Trade Commission Act declares unlawful "unfair methods of competition" and "unfair deceptive acts or practices." The FTC has been granted authority to promulgate rules and regulations interpreting the provisions of this Act. Pursuant to such authority, it has created many rules and regulations that proscribe misleading or confusing advertising practices, some of which place affirmative duties of disclosure upon the manufacturers of products. Both the FTC and private parties may take enforcement measures against violations.

Moreover, many of the individual states have enacted statutes that similarly prohibit unfair competition; these state statutes are also enforceable by either the state or private parties.

Restraint of Competition (Antitrust)

Compliance with US antitrust laws impacts a number of distribution and marketing issues. A sample of the different issues facing a foreign company includes:

1. Territorial and Customer Restrictions: Although a manufacturer may assign a specific territory to a distributor, it may be illegal to prohibit a distributor from selling the manufacturer's products outside the assigned territory. Such limitations are not automatically illegal, but will be weighed as to their reasonableness in light of all relevant facts and circumstances.

2. Pricing: A manufacturer may not establish the prices at which its distributors resell its products. However, manufacturers are free to "suggest" resale prices or even unilaterally refuse to do business with a distributor that fails to comply with these suggested prices.

3. Product Supply: A requirement that a distributor obtain its entire supply of a particular product from the manufacturer (or similarly, refrain from handling any products that compete with the manufacturer's products) may violate US antitrust law if the

arrangement restricts a "substantial amount of trade." A violation will occur if the manufacturer or distributor is a significant player in a concentrated market.

The foregoing limitations generally do not impact foreign companies conducting business through a sales representative.

Customs and Import Procedures

The Bureau of Customs and Border Protection, or CBP, which is part of the Department of Homeland Security, enforces all laws relating to goods crossing the US border.

When goods are imported into the United States, there must be a formal "importer of record" who is responsible for complying with applicable laws and paying all customs duties and fees. US law allows a non-resident company to be the importer of record. However, it is typically in a foreign seller's interest for the US distributor or customer to be the importer of record, because the foreign seller then avoids the burdens of complying with applicable laws and paying customs duties and fees.

Which party is the importer of record is a matter of party agreement, and this is usually covered by the delivery term specified in the governing sale-of-goods contract.

While any importer has the right to prepare and file a customs entry for goods that it imports, a commercial importer typically hires a customs broker to file customs entries on behalf of the importer. Only a customs broker, fully licensed by CBP, may act as an importer's agent in this capacity. US law requires an importer to execute a power of attorney appointing a customs broker as attorney-in-fact.

However, an importer remains liable vis-à-vis CBP for any errors committed by a customs broker when it prepares import paperwork on behalf of the importer.

Also, a commercial importer will need to obtain a customs bond from a surety company. This bond is a third-party guarantee for payment of duties and certain penalties associated with any violations of US import laws.

While there are hundreds of US laws that may apply to any given importation of goods, there are three main areas of substantive customs law with which an importer must comply:
- Classification
- Valuation
- Marking

All imported goods must be classified in the Harmonized Tariff Schedule of the United States, and classification is the chief determinant of the applicable duty rate.

All imported goods must be valued in accordance with applicable law, which in many cases will be based on the price paid or payable for the goods. Because most duty rates are expressed as a percentage of the import value, applicable customs duties are typically determined by the combination of duty rate, as provided by a product's classification, and import value.

Finally, almost all imported goods must bear a country-of-origin marking, in English, so that the ultimate US purchaser of a product is made aware of the product's origin.

An importer must take seriously its compliance with the import-related laws of the United States. Before 1994, an importer only needed to provide the US government with the correct facts concerning the products being imported.

Since 1994, however, an importer has also been required to understand and apply certain law to the facts in order to, for example, determine the correct classification and value of imported goods. The role of the CBP is to confirm the correctness of such determinations made by the importer. In this regulatory structure, compliance with law is essentially shifted, at least in the first instance, to the importer itself; and an importer may be assessed penalties if it does not use reasonable care to understand the facts or law or when it applies the law to the facts.

Chapter 24: Acquisitions

There has historically existed in the United States a strong tendency to establish new enterprises, which have been the source of much of the growth in the US economy over at least the last decade. Eventually, investors in these enterprises seek to liquidate their interests, often through a sale to a larger company. The result of this dynamic has led to a vibrant US market in business enterprises.

Acquiring a business enterprise is also an attractive possibility for established companies. The target enterprise will typically have overcome most start-up risks. While this will understandably be reflected in a higher price, the buyer will acquire a going concern, with all of its personnel and assets, and usually a profitable operation as well.

The advantages of having in place senior managers experienced in the US market, thereby overcoming the principal cultural impediment to entering the US economy, is often a factor that is particularly appealing to non-US investors when contemplating entering the US market via acquisition of an existing business.

As might be expected from the foregoing, the US market for business enterprises is highly developed. It affords the knowledgeable buyer the opportunity to learn about the target enterprise in depth before buying to reduce the risk of post-closing surprises so common elsewhere.

Moreover, US buyers use sophisticated documentation to precisely allocate the risks of the business between buyer and seller and to protect the seller against undisclosed liabilities.

To take full advantage of these opportunities, a non-US investor will benefit from highly experienced legal and other advisors, beginning in the earliest planning stages of an acquisition. Moreover, those advisors need to be able to explain and interpret the acquisition process in terms that can be fully understood by a buyer from another country.

Acquisitions documents are intended to be comprehensive, and each would need to be appropriately tailored to the particular transaction, but they provide an overview of some of the key issues typically considered by buyers at the outset of an acquisition.

- Regulatory Framework
- Governmental Approvals
- General

Foreign acquisitions of US businesses are assisted by a general absence of exchange controls, government regulation, or licensing of foreign investment or foreign acquisitions in the United States. Foreign-owned enterprises also have equal access to federal and state investment incentives and benefits, except as noted below.

Many states have offered significant tax and other incentives to induce non-US manufacturers of automobiles and other items to establish facilities in such states. However, foreign-owned enterprises and certain acquisitions of US companies by non-US entities are subject to some regulations and reporting requirements.

Exon-Florio

The Exon-Florio provision of the 1988 Omnibus Trade and Competitiveness Act authorizes the President of the United States to review certain acquisitions, mergers, and takeovers of US companies or businesses by non-US entities. It applies to any transaction that could result in non-US "control" of a US person or entity. This includes the power to make significant decisions, even where only a minority interest is acquired.

The US President is empowered to suspend or prohibit any such acquisition, or order divestment of the acquired company if the acquisition has been completed, if the President finds credible evidence that the non-US person might take any action that threatens to impair US national security. The US President has delegated the authority to investigate to the Committee on Foreign Investment in the United States, or CFIUS, an interagency group.

The definition of national security has been left vague, listing just three factors to consider in making a determination:
1. The domestic production needed for projected national defence requirements.
2. The capability and capacity of domestic industries to meet national defence requirements, including the availability of human resources, products, technology, materials, and other supplies and services.
3. The control of domestic industries and commercial activity by non-US citizens as it affects the capability and capacity of the United States to meet the requirements of national security.

The last factor could be interpreted to include even non-defence industries, and many acquisitions of companies having no connection to the defence industry have been reported to CFIUS.

The Exon-Florio provisions impose strict time limits for the investigation and review procedures. Review will begin upon receipt by CFIUS of either "voluntary" notice from the parties involved or notice from an appropriate agency of the US government.

This notice must contain a significant amount of prescribed information, including the latest available transaction documents. CFIUS has 30 days to decide whether the transaction should be investigated. If CFIUS finds that an investigation is warranted, it has 45 days to conduct the investigation, during which it may request additional documents and personal appearances by the parties, and make its decision.

An investigation is mandatory where a foreign government-controlled entity acquires control of a US company and CFIUS concludes that the transaction "could affect national security." The US President then has 15 days to review and approve the decision. Transactions will be allowed to proceed without interference unless action is taken by the government within these time periods. However, unreported transactions will continue to be subject to review at any time. Therefore, in case of doubt, it will make sense to report any sizable transaction to CFIUS before proceeding with an acquisition.

In July 2006, the US Congress proposed several changes to the review process, which are still pending as of the date of this publication.

Chapter 25: Exchange Controls and Report

The United States exercises few controls over foreign exchange transactions by US citizens or non-US persons. No approval of the US Department of Treasury or other finance authority is required to make an investment.

Subject to applicable tax rules, a foreign-owned enterprise is free to invest capital and to remit profits, repatriate capital and pay interest and royalties to a non-US parent without any license or restriction. However, the US government monitors foreign exchange transactions of substantial size. Although this monitoring is only for informational purposes, failure to make full and accurate disclosure where required could result in serious criminal penalties under money-laundering and other federal statutes.

Foreign-owned enterprises are required to make periodic, direct investment reports to the US Department of Commerce pursuant to the International Investment Survey Act of 1976 if 10% or more of a substantial enterprise is foreign-owned.

Investment by non-US persons in real estate requires additional reports, particularly to US tax authorities, under the Foreign Investment in Real Property Tax Act.

The acquisition and transfer of agricultural land must be reported to the US Department of Agriculture. Real estate acquisitions may also give rise to other, non-federal, reporting obligations.

A non-US buyer of industrial property in a rural area should be careful to ascertain whether any portion of the property purchased can be considered agricultural property, but no specific report is necessary for acquisition of non-agricultural land.

Chapter 26: Restricted Industries

Ownership by non-US persons of certain restricted industries is limited or regulated by the federal government or some state governments.

Restricted industries include the defence, banking, insurance, domestic air or water transportation, fishing, radio and television broadcasting industries and in some states the railroad industry and agricultural and other real estate.

A non-US buyer contemplating a purchase of a company in one of these industries should consult with US legal counsel at the earliest possible stage about potential restrictions.

Banking is an example of a US industry regulated at both the state and federal levels. A non-US bank may establish either a federal or state-chartered branch to engage in banking directly, a federal or state-chartered agency to engage in more limited international banking services, or a state-chartered representative office to provide limited representation and administrative services in the United States for the foreign bank.

The establishment of any such office requires approval by the Federal Reserve Board and, in the case of a state-chartered entity, approval by the relevant state banking authorities. Once licensed, such branch, agency or representative office is subject to on-going prudential supervision by its regulators in the United States.

In addition, a foreign bank wishing to take retail deposits (initial deposits of less than $100,000) in the United States can only do so by obtaining approval for establishing a US subsidiary bank meeting the requirements of the Federal Deposit Insurance Corporation (FDIC) for insured deposits.

A non-US bank may also acquire an existing US bank provided it obtains approval of the federal banking authorities and, if the target bank is state-chartered, approval of the relevant state banking authorities. Most state laws do not restrict foreign ownership of state-chartered banks, and state regulatory authorities are increasingly willing to approve takeovers by foreign banks; no state approvals are required, however, in respect of the acquisition of a federally-chartered bank.

In establishing a branch or agency in the United States, a foreign bank must satisfy the Federal Reserve Board that it is principally engaged in the business of banking (rather than in manufacturing or other commercial activities), that it is subject to comprehensive consolidated supervision by its home country regulator, and that it meets various other requirements related to its financial condition, its anti-money laundering practices and US regulators' access to information on an ongoing basis in respect of their prudential supervision of such branch or agency.

Upon a foreign bank's establishment of a US branch or agency, its direct and indirect activities and investments in the United States (including non-banking commercial activities and investments) must meet standards established by the Federal Reserve Board.

Similar requirements must be met in the case of a foreign bank's acquisition of a US bank. A foreign bank acquiring or establishing a US bank must obtain approval from the Federal

94

Reserve Board to become a bank holding company which requires, among many other factors, a determination that the foreign bank is subject to comprehensive consolidated supervision by its home country regulator.

The Gramm-Leach-Bliley Act of 1999 significantly expanded the non-banking activities in which banks, including non-US banks, can engage (e.g., insurance, merchant banking and other financial activities) provided that such institutions qualify both as bank holding companies and financial holding companies. Banks in the United States, however, are still generally prohibited from engaging in commercial activities.

A non-US bank's worldwide structure and long-range plans should be examined in detail before it attempts to establish a presence in the United States or to acquire a US bank.

Chapter 27: Antitrust Regulations

Other legal matters that a non-US buyer must consider in connection with an acquisition of a US company include antitrust notification requirements, federal and state securities regulations, and regulations regarding mergers.

US antitrust law prohibits any acquisition or merger that would have the tendency to lessen competition or create a monopoly. However, this restriction has rarely been used to block acquisitions if the buyer is foreign and has no, or limited, existing operations in the United States.

If a US acquisition meets certain minimum size levels, a Hart-Scott-Rodino pre-merger notification must be filed with the US Department of Justice and the Federal Trade Commission, or FTC. (The filing thresholds are revised periodically but as of the date of the publication of this book, in general, a filing is required for acquisitions having a value of $226.8 million or more without regard to the size of the parties involved; or a value of less than $56.7 million if the parties are of a certain size.)

Detailed financial and descriptive information concerning the ultimate parent of the acquiring and target corporations, their product lines, and the transaction itself must be included. The ultimate parent will be the corporation that is highest in the chain of ownership if the actual buyer is a subsidiary. If the ultimate parent corporation is privately owned (as would be the case with many family-owned enterprises), the ultimate parent may be the family itself. Although the notification may appear burdensome and unnecessarily intrusive, buyers can normally comply with the law by disclosing only a reasonable amount of business information.

The parties must wait 30 days after the filing to complete the acquisition, although early termination of the waiting period may be requested. It is not permissible to proceed with the acquisition prior to expiration of the waiting period even if the transaction is made expressly subject to divestment in case the government later objects.

Managerial and financial control of the target must remain with the seller until expiration of the waiting period. However, the effective date of the acquisition may be made retroactive to a date prior to such expiration, thereby giving the buyer the financial benefit of the target company's operations during the waiting period if the transaction ultimately proceeds.

The Department of Justice or FTC may request additional information at any time during the waiting period, in which case the waiting period will be suspended until the information is provided. Such a second request can be very burdensome and time consuming. Therefore, the parties are usually quite willing to discuss the transaction and provide additional information to the government to avoid a second request. Parties should ensure that all information provided is accurate and complete, especially if the timing of the acquisition is important. Hart-Scott-Rodino filings are confidential. US government authorities will not even confirm or deny if a filing has been made (unless the parties have requested an early termination of the waiting period). Therefore, filing a notification generally should not jeopardize an acquisition or create unwanted publicity in the United States or in the buyer's home country.

Chapter 28: Securities Laws

The purchase and sale of securities, including the shares of a corporation and ownership interests in many other entities, are strictly regulated by both federal and state governments.

Issuance of Shares

A non-US corporation may issue shares or other securities in the United States to finance an acquisition, for example by exchanging its shares for the shares or assets of the target company. However, the shares or other securities must be issued pursuant to a registration statement filed with the SEC (containing or incorporating detailed information regarding the issuer's business affairs and financial condition), unless an exemption from registration is available. The most commonly used exemption in acquisitions is the private offering exemption, that is, an offering to a limited number of sophisticated investors.

In many cases, the buyer is required to make full disclosure concerning its business affairs and financial condition to the seller if it issues securities to the seller, even in certain private transactions. Strict antifraud provisions apply to any issuance or sale of shares or other securities.

Tender Offers

A tender offer is subject to regulation under federal securities law, including the antifraud rules. As a threshold matter, a notice must be filed with the SEC once more than 5% of any class of a publicly held target's securities are acquired. It must include a statement of the purchaser's intentions.

A detailed discussion of the rules that apply to tender offers is beyond the scope of this book. However, effective December 2006, the SEC amended the so-called "best price rule" for tender offers to, among other things, make it clear that the rule does not apply to consideration offered and paid to employees and directors of the target company in accordance with compensation, severance or other employee benefit arrangements.

These amendments clarify the tender offer process and should put tender offers on more equal footing with other forms of business combinations, including mergers, as a means for structuring acquisitions of US publicly-held companies.

Certain states have adopted legislation to make hostile tender offers to domiciliaries more difficult. Furthermore, corporations have adopted restrictions in their articles of incorporation and have taken other defensive measures for the same purpose.

Mergers

A merger is a joining together of two or more corporations by operation of law.

A non-US buyer will not merge directly with the target but will typically establish a US subsidiary to act as the merger partner. A merger with a public company will require the approval of the target's stockholders and so will be subject to securities law regulations.

Public stockholder approval must be obtained through a proxy statement that must contain certain prescribed information, including financial information on the proposed merger partner and often on its non-US parent.

Chapter 29: Structuring an Acquisition

Many factors must be considered in structuring the acquisition. Many of these apply in domestic transactions, although they tend to be more complicated in a cross-border acquisition.

Shares or Cash

The use of cash to acquire shares or assets or to effect a merger offers no legal difficulties. This is the form normally used by a non-US buyer. There may be tax advantages (especially to the sellers) to using shares or other securities to acquire the shares or assets of a target enterprise.

The use of shares for this purpose is subject to securities law regulation. As noted above, shares or other securities may be issued only pursuant to a registration statement unless an exemption from registration is available. In addition, the target's stockholders will be interested in taking shares only if there is a significant public market for the shares offered.

This limitation severely hinders the possibility of non-US buyers using shares unless they have shares or other securities traded on a US stock exchange or on NASDAQ, including perhaps US Depository Receipts, or ADRs, or the seller is willing to accept securities traded on a foreign exchange.

Acquisition Vehicle

A non-US buyer may acquire shares or assets directly. As noted above, more often, a non-US buyer will establish a US acquisition vehicle in the form of a partnership or corporation to acquire assets and, often, shares.

Partnership

A US partnership may be a general partnership, with unlimited liability for all partners, or a limited partnership, with limited liability for the limited partners.

Corporations may be partners in either type of partnership. A partnership will often be used if the acquired business is to be conducted as a joint venture, since such a structure may offer tax advantages for both US and non-US participants.

A partnership may be used if the target business primarily involves real estate or natural resources. An investment in partnership form may also have advantages for investors from certain countries, such as Germany, where income earned through a US partnership might not be subject to taxation outside of the United States.

Limited Liability Companies

Limited liability companies have come into use in the United States fairly recently but are now used regularly in place of corporations in US practice.

A limited liability company offers the informality of a partnership while (as the name implies) providing a limitation on the liability of all of the members to their investment in the company. A limited liability company may be structured so as to be taxed in the United States as if it were a partnership, which can be very advantageous to a non-US acquirer. A limited liability company is also very attractive for joint ventures or any situation in which the target is to be owned by two or more unrelated parties.

Corporation

A corporation is the traditional acquisition vehicle used by non-US buyers. The corporation is the only form of share company in the United States. A corporation may be organized in any state, territory or the District of Columbia. A US corporation may be organized very quickly, since organization does not require prior approval of any governmental authority or involve prolonged review or processing of documents or outside valuation of contributions.

There is no limitation on non-US persons acting as stockholders in a US corporation except for certain regulated industries discussed earlier in this book.

Holding Company

A new corporation or limited liability company may be used to acquire shares, thereby establishing a holding company structure. A US holding company may be used if assets are to be acquired or if the acquisition is to be effected through a merger. Such a structure is permissible and comparatively simple in the United States, since a US corporation and most limited liability companies may have a single stockholder or member.

US corporate members of the corporate group may file a consolidated income tax return. A holding company structure is likely to give the non-US buyer greater flexibility in tax and business planning in the future, especially if it plans to make other US acquisitions.

Share Acquisitions

The acquisition of shares or membership interests is the simplest form of acquisition, especially if there are only a few stockholders and all are willing to sell. As in any other sale of securities, the seller will be subject to the antifraud provisions of US securities law, but it is customary to include the same full set of disclosure provisions in either a share or an asset acquisition agreement.

Advantages

Where shares are acquired, all assets remain in the target company and few transfer documents are required. Thus, the acquisition may be completed fairly quickly, even if a public tender offer is required. Transfer taxes may also be limited or avoided, although such taxes are relatively low in most states (Florida is an exception for real estate), so using a share acquisition for the purpose of avoiding transfer taxes is generally less of a concern in the United States compared to many other countries.

The target company will retain all of its assets, including its licenses, permits, and franchises. In an asset transaction, these can be difficult to transfer because of the need to obtain consents from the issuing government agencies. In a share acquisition, important contracts and leases may be unaffected by the transfer. These matters must be investigated, however, to make certain that a change of control of the target will not bring about termination of permits or contracts.

Disadvantages

In a share acquisition, the target company will usually retain its tax attributes, both favourable and unfavourable, assuming that the business is continued.

There are, however, limitations on the future use of some attributes, such as net operating losses. A higher purchase price paid for the business may not be reflected in the tax basis of the target corporation's assets after the acquisition, unless the seller consents to certain elections.

Since these elections are usually disadvantageous to the seller, they are rarely made where the seller is a US taxpayer. The target company will retain all of its tax and other liabilities, whether disclosed or undisclosed, although, in a US transaction, the seller will typically indemnify the buyer against any undisclosed liability of the target.

A share acquisition can also be cumbersome if the buyer does not wish to purchase the target company in its entirety. In certain cases it may be possible for the target to rid itself of the unwanted business or assets prior to a share acquisition. However, both the legal and tax aspects of a de-merger (or corporate split) are complicated in the United States.

Advantages of Asset Acquisitions

If assets are acquired, the buyer's tax basis in the assets may be increased to reflect the actual purchase price. Also, not all the assets of the target company need be purchased. Thus, if one is interested in only one line of business or one division of a corporation, an asset purchase is the most straightforward way to accomplish the transaction.

107

Another benefit of an asset acquisition is that not all liabilities need be acquired. However, certain liabilities may pass to the acquirer in any case. For example, certain state property taxes will constitute a lien on the assets acquired.

Environmental liabilities may become the responsibility of any subsequent owner.

Substantial pension liabilities may pass to the purchaser under some circumstances.

A few states will impose responsibility on the acquiring company for product liability claims even for products sold prior to the acquisition. In the United States, the seller will usually indemnify the buyer against any such liabilities in the acquisition agreement, which may be sufficient protection if the seller is financially sound.

In a few states, assets may also remain subject to attachment by creditors of the seller for a period of time after the transaction is closed unless certain bulk sales procedures, including notices to all creditors of the seller, are followed.

These procedures are quite inconvenient and are often ignored when the seller is a substantial corporation, in which case the buyer will rely on the seller's indemnification against any claims of creditors. A number of states have abolished such bulk sales laws. If the selling company is insolvent, great care must be taken to avoid any charge of fraudulent conveyance, that is, a disposition of assets for inadequate consideration while a company is insolvent or that causes it to become so. Fraudulent conveyance can be actionable by a company's creditors.

Disadvantages

Favourable tax attributes of the target corporation will normally be lost in an asset acquisition. An asset acquisition is also more complex than a share acquisition because all assets must be transferred. Consents to the transfer of certain valuable assets, such as licenses, permits, or contracts, may not be obtainable or may be obtainable only at a significant price. However, it is not usually difficult to obtain consents from public or private parties merely because the ultimate buyer is a non-US person.

Mergers

All state laws provide for the merger of corporations and most states now provide for the merger of limited liability companies and other entities (including a merger of different forms of entity). In a merger, two entities are joined by operation of law, that is, all assets and liabilities become the property of the surviving entity (or a new entity) solely by filing a certificate of merger.

Normally, one entity disappears and the other continues as the successor to both lines of business. To be effective, a merger requires the consent of the board of directors and stockholders (in a corporation) or the members (in a limited liability company) and a public filing with the state. Any form of consideration may be used in a merger.

Thus, equity interests in the target may be converted to cash, to equity interests in the acquiring entity, or to equity interests in any other entity. The target entity may also be the survivor, often termed a reverse merger. In this case, it is still possible to eliminate the target's stockholders by automatically converting their shares to cash or to shares in the buyer or any other corporation.

Advantages

The principal advantage of a merger is that the transfer of assets and the exchange of target corporation shares are automatic. Stockholders of the target corporation have no option to retain their shares (although dissenting stockholders may have the right to obtain an appraisal of their shares and recover the appraised value in lieu of the amount offered to them in the merger). No separate transfer documents are required.

Transfer taxes normally do not apply in a merger.

Valuable permits, contracts, and the like may also be easier to transfer in a merger than in an asset sale, but these do not remain in the same corporate entity unless the merger is accomplished through a reverse merger.

Disadvantages

A merger with a publicly held corporation may be time consuming because of the need to hold a meeting of the stockholders and to comply with US proxy rules.

If the publicly held target is attractive to other potential bidders, the delay in effecting a merger may allow these other bidders to compete for the target, increasing the price of the shares and, possibly, frustrating the acquisition. While contested takeovers have become more common in Europe in recent years, non-US clients are often reluctant to battle, or even compete, with other bidders. In such cases, a friendly tender offer for sufficient shares to approve a merger may be effective.

This process may be completed quickly. If the tender is successful, timing will no longer be important, and any remaining stockholders can be eliminated through a "cash out" merger of the acquisition vehicle with the target.

Financing an Acquisition

It is increasingly common to finance an acquisition with the target's assets or future profits. This method is called a leveraged buyout. The assets of the target company may be pledged to a bank or other financial institution, or the buyer may issue high interest, subordinated debt instruments, normally referred to as junk bonds.

Such bonds constitute securities and must be registered with the SEC unless an exemption from registration is available. Unlike the case under many European corporate laws, the use of the target's assets to finance the acquisition is not illegal or even disreputable in the United States. Nonetheless, non-US buyers rarely use local US debt financing (leveraged or otherwise) for an acquisition, although this is affected by interest rates in the United States.

Non-US buyers are more likely to use stockholder loans to finance an acquisition, especially if they have borrowed in their own countries. This approach is another form of leveraged buyout, since it is the target that will effectively repay the borrowing. Since dividends are not deductible by the US target payor, it is generally advantageous to treat payments to non-US stockholders as interest. However, such loans must bear a US market interest rate, be treated as loans, and not constitute too great a portion of the company's financing versus its share capital. Interest payments (and dividends) to non-US persons may be subject to US withholding tax.

Chapter 30: Investigating the Target Company

In the United States, it is generally assumed that the buyer of a company is entitled to complete information regarding the company, its operations, financial situation, and prospects.

This information is typically acquired in two ways.

First, at the very outset of the transaction, often prior to the execution of a letter of intent, the potential buyer will provide to the seller an extensive list of information and documentation that it wishes to examine.

This will usually be supplemented by inquiries focused on the specific target company. This process is generally referred to as "due diligence."

The information requested will cover all aspects of the target business, including the legal organization of the target company, its financial condition, its principal contracts, its environmental condition, its employment and employee benefit compliance, and the like.

Since the information that will be produced will be similarly broad, it may be examined and analyzed not only by the buyer and its legal counsel but also by its other advisors, particularly its investment bankers, if any, and its accountants. Furthermore, these other advisors may supplement the legal due diligence request with requests for information of particular interest to them.

Second, the information produced in the due diligence process often will be supplemented and confirmed through the representations and warranties in the acquisition agreement itself.

These representations and warranties will constitute factual statements about the target company. Any exceptions to those statements will have to be disclosed in schedules to the agreement. Certain representations and warranties will call for affirmative disclosures.

Thus, the information provided in a due diligence process often will become a contractual guaranty and undertaking on the part of the seller for which the seller may be liable in damages in the event that any of the representations or other information is incorrect.

Chapter 31: Acquisition Documents

Letter of Intent

The letter of intent sets out the principal points upon which the parties have reached tentative agreement. It is useful in identifying important issues between the parties.

Its disadvantages are that it may delay the preparation and signing of a definitive contract and, in the case of public companies, prematurely trigger the need for public disclosure of the transaction.

Except for certain matters, such as confidentiality, standstill, and the like, a letter of intent is typically not legally binding between the parties. However, a US party will be most reluctant to make important changes in the terms set out in the letter of intent absent a significant change in the target or in the circumstances of the transaction. A letter of intent may also create legal liabilities if one of the parties fails to negotiate the definitive agreement in good faith. Finally, the letter of intent may address significant matters, such as limitations on the liability of the seller that should be carefully analyzed before being agreed to. Thus, it is important that all matters of importance to the non-US buyer, especially the material terms and the structure of the transaction, be considered and reviewed with legal counsel before a letter of intent is signed.

Acquisition Agreement

With or without a letter of intent, the parties and their attorneys must prepare and negotiate a definitive acquisition agreement. It should set out all of the rights and obligations of the parties, both before and after the closing. A non-US buyer should expect an explanation of all aspects of the acquisition agreement, since that is typically the key document setting forth the allocation of risks between the parties.

A non-US buyer should never fear to appear unsophisticated and should take nothing for granted. Many non-US buyers make unwarranted assumptions based on business and legal practices in their own countries. Lawyers should try to explain all elements of the acquisition agreement and related agreements in terms that take into account the buyer's own experience and draft documents that make the terms of agreement easier for the client to understand, avoiding unnecessary legalese or lawyer's terminology. Nonetheless, questions from clients are always appropriate and welcome.

Acquisition agreements in the United States tend to be fairly long. The principal features of a US acquisition agreement are described below.

Subject of Acquisition

The property to be acquired by the buyer, whether assets, shares, or a combination of both, should be specified. Any assets or business to be excluded must also be identified. If a merger is contemplated, this will be described.

Price

The price paid for a US enterprise may be fixed, subject to adjustment, or contingent.

The cash price in a share acquisition or merger may be fixed, although the seller may represent that the target's net working capital, or other financial statement or operating item, will be a certain minimum, with post-closing downward, or sometimes upward, adjustments to the price for amounts above or below such minimum figure. Net working capital or other measuring rods are often determined by a post-closing audit. Such audits, usually conducted by an independent accounting firm, are quite customary in the United States and would only rarely be resisted by a US seller. An audit affords the non-US buyer substantial protection, but an audit should only supplement the buyer's own pre-closing due diligence investigation.

In an asset transaction, the seller's cash is normally excluded. The price paid for property, plant and equipment, and non-balance sheet intangibles, such as intellectual property or good will, will be fixed, but the price for current assets, particularly inventory and receivables, will depend on the level of such assets as of the closing.

These and any other items subject to adjustment are often determined by an audit conducted immediately after the closing.

If a target's earnings history is short or subject to question, the parties may make part of the purchase price contingent on future earnings performance. Such an earn-out arrangement is fraught with difficulty, since the buyer wishes to operate the purchased business freely, but the seller will have a continuing interest in it and therefore wishes to impose significant limitations on the buyer.

Allocation of Price

In an asset transaction it is advantageous to allocate the purchase price to specific assets so as to avoid the parties' taking inconsistent positions. The parties will normally agree to use these allocations for all tax purposes. The parties are not completely free to make any allocation they wish, for allocations are subject to challenge by tax authorities, who have an interest in allocating as much of the purchase price as possible to non-depreciable items or items depreciable only over long periods, such as goodwill.

Payment

An acquisition agreement normally calls for payment by wire transfer at the closing, although bank (cashier's) checks are sometimes used.

A portion of the price may be paid on a deferred basis through the issuance of a promissory note. This will permit the purchase to be more easily financed out of the assets and future profits of the acquired business. It may also provide a means for satisfying any claims that the buyer may have after the closing. A portion of the purchase price may also be placed in an escrow account established with a bank or other third party. The funds are held in the account for an agreed period of time and disbursed to satisfy buyer's claims after the closing. A non-US buyer should always consider these alternatives, even though they may not be customary in the buyer's own country.

Assumption of Liabilities

In a sense, all liabilities are assumed in a share transaction or merger, since after the closing the buyer will own the debtor corporation or a successor in interest to it.

Normally, only the target's assets are exposed to such liabilities, although this may be of little solace to the buyer if undisclosed liabilities appear after the closing. As noted earlier in this book, this risk is somewhat mitigated by the seller's indemnity against any undisclosed liabilities that one customarily finds in US acquisition agreements.

In an asset acquisition, the liabilities to be assumed and excluded should be described in considerable detail. The buyer will have to assume post-closing obligations under all contracts assigned to it but should expressly exclude pre-closing breaches of those contracts.

The buyer should also consider assuming trade payables, since it is the buyer who will have the greatest interest in seeing that suppliers of goods and services are paid. The amount of the liabilities assumed should be considered a part of the overall purchase price. Generally, liabilities not specifically assumed by the buyer are retained by the seller.

Representations and Warranties

Representations and warranties are usually quite extensive and cover the areas of greatest concern to the parties.

Acquisitions in the United States are made on the basis of full disclosure of all aspects of the purchased business.

Representations and warranties are primarily designed to provide disclosure of information about the target enterprise but, they, along with the indemnification provisions, also allocate the risks of the business between the parties and can form the basis of claims after the closing.

Covenants

In a typical acquisition of a US enterprise, the acquisition agreement is negotiated several weeks (or more) prior to the actual closing, when the business and consideration changes hands. Any matters to be carried out between the signing of the contract and the closing (or beyond it) will be set forth as the specific covenants of one party to another.

One of the most significant covenants, therefore, is that which requires the seller to conduct the business in the ordinary course between contract and closing. It will typically prohibit the seller from engaging in any major transactions without the advance approval of the buyer, and the obtaining of any key consents or approvals to the transactions.

Conditions

The preconditions to closing the transaction will be set forth in the acquisition agreement. Typically, conditions are included as to the continued accuracy of the seller's representations and warranties, the performance of the seller's covenants, the rendering of legal opinions, the execution of ancillary agreements, the absence of any material adverse change in the seller's business, and the obtaining of any key consents or approvals to the transaction.

Closing

The transfer documents to be executed and delivered at the closing, as well as the method of payment of the purchase price, should be specified.

Indemnification

An indemnity is a form of guaranty under which one party undertakes to reimburse another party for a specified loss or liability the other party may suffer. Insurance is a common form of indemnification. Indemnity provisions are commonly used in the United States to allocate risks of a target business between seller and buyer.

If a public company is acquired, it is impractical in most cases to obtain any continuing indemnity from the public stockholders after the closing, and the target's management and controlling stockholders, if any, will generally refuse to accept the responsibility alone. In this situation, the representations and warranties will expire at the closing and there will be no ongoing indemnity obligation. The burden is on the buyer to verify all facts about the target before closing. The buyer will be aided in this by the fact that the target has been subject to the public disclosure obligations of US securities law.

If the target is privately owned, the acquisition agreement typically will require the seller to indemnify the buyer for any misrepresentations, or breaches of warranties or covenants. The buyer will be subject to a similar obligation in favour of the seller.

The indemnification provisions will allocate responsibility for liabilities or losses arising from the conduct of the business both before and after the closing. An indemnification provision will also specify the period following the closing during which the seller will be responsible to the other party. The parties have a natural desire to end their indemnification obligations as soon as possible.

"Survival" periods are typically between one and three years, but one full year of operation plus a complete audit of such year are essential (and often sufficient) to identify possible indemnification claims.

Environmental indemnification obligations and claims with respect to title to the shares or membership interests or, perhaps, assets are often unlimited in time.

Indemnification provisions may specify that claims may be made only after the aggregate amount of all claims reaches a certain minimum level. Once this level is reached, the agreement may permit a party to assert all claims or only those in excess of the minimum. It is increasingly common for an agreement to provide a maximum for claims that may be asserted, typically with carve-outs from this amount for various matters including taxes, capitalization, intentional misrepresentation and fraud.

Other Agreements

The acquisition agreement may provide for a variety of ancillary agreements to be signed at the closing. These may include non-competition agreements, employment agreements with one or more of the sellers or key employees of the target, and ongoing leases and licenses.

Chapter 32: Representations and Warranties

The representations and warranties in the acquisition agreement focus on matters of great legal and business concern to the buyer.

Representations and warranties are designed to elicit information about the target company. Thus, they play a vital role in the buyer's investigation of the target.

The disclosures made in the acquisition agreement will be based in part on the due diligence investigation performed by counsel and others for the seller and will be further verified by the investigation of the buyer and its counsel. This investigation may be more far-reaching than would be encountered in the non-US buyer's home country.

The expense involved should be weighed against the added protection afforded the buyer. Each acquisition agreement will be tailored to the particular transaction and, accordingly, the scope of the representations and warranties will vary from deal to deal.

The following is a general discussion of some of the more common representations and warranties that often appear in a US acquisition agreement.

Corporate Authority and Organization

The seller will represent that the selling entity is properly organized and that the persons acting on its behalf are duly authorized to do so. There is no commercial register or the equivalent in the United States. Therefore, the buyer and its counsel typically will independently verify the seller's authority through examination of the target's books and records, as well as public filings of publicly held targets, and may also obtain a legal opinion from the seller's counsel concerning the seller's and target company's organization and authorization.

Financial Statements

The acquisition agreement will state that the financial statements that have been presented to the buyer (which may or may not be attached to the agreement) have been prepared in accordance with generally accepted accounting principles on a basis consistent with prior periods and "fairly present" the financial condition of the target.

Financial representations will be included even if all financial statements have been audited by a reputable accounting firm. They may also be supplemented by specific representations as to certain assets, such as inventory and accounts receivable. Where the buyer is subject to the Sarbanes-Oxley Act, representations may also be included with respect to internal controls and certification requirements arising under this particular law.

Chapter 33: Compliance with Law

Environmental Compliance

In the United States, the buyer will inherit legal responsibility for any environmental problems existing on any property purchased, whether the transaction is in the form of an asset acquisition, share acquisition, or merger.

Environmental liabilities represent one of the most significant traps for the unwary buyer. Therefore, buyers typically want full disclosure of any such problems. These will include any failure by the business to comply with environmental laws or any environmental permits for day-to-day operations.

Of equal concern are any hazardous waste materials that may be stored or buried on any real property. The removal of such waste can be very expensive. In many industries, it may be appropriate to have a so-called Phase I environmental audit of the premises and, if problems appear, a Phase II or Phase III audit that includes soil borings and air and water tests, to ascertain the presence and extent of any such problems. (However, Phase II and III environmental audits may trigger disclosure obligations.) The buyer will want to confirm that any waste materials that have been carried off the premises have been handled and disposed of in accordance with applicable legal requirements.

A purchaser may become liable for the improper off-site disposal of waste material by a predecessor or even by an unrelated third party, such as a waste disposal service retained by a previous owner of the business.

Environmental permits or licenses will have to be transferred or new ones obtained in the case of an asset acquisition. It will be necessary to consult with environmental authorities to be certain that the permits will be respected upon the change of ownership in a share acquisition.

In certain states, such as New Jersey and Connecticut, the advance approval of state authorities may be required in order to complete the acquisition. Because environmental liabilities are so extensive in scope, buyers often seek to make the seller's environmental indemnities unlimited in monetary amount and time.

Other Licenses and Permits

Although the regulation of businesses is relatively limited in the United States, most businesses operate with a variety of governmental licenses and permits. These include general business licenses; building permits and certificates of occupancy relating to structures; boiler permits and other permits to operate certain forms of machinery and equipment; and vehicle licenses and registrations.

In addition, specific governmental licenses and franchises may be necessary for certain kinds of businesses. It may be possible to transfer these license and permits to the buyer in an asset acquisition.

More often, however, new license and permits should be obtained. Arrangements for the transfer or obtaining of such licenses or permits must be made so that they are in place at the closing if the business is to continue without interruption. Even vehicle registrations may present problems, since their transfer may take some time.

Government licenses and permits are generally not assignable even though material to the business. They may also terminate in the event of a material change in control of the target. The latter is more often imposed by practice on the local level than by statute. In such case, the buyer will want to be certain it can obtain its own licenses and permits prior to the closing. The agreement will generally call for disclosure of the licenses and permits used by the business and have a representation as to assignability.

Compliance with Other Laws

The buyer typically will wish to confirm that the business operates in compliance with zoning laws and other local laws regulating the use of real estate. Zoning law compliance is not always covered by title insurance. The buyer likely will be concerned about compliance with federal occupational safety and health laws. It is unlikely that the seller will be able to give absolute assurance of such compliance, but the buyer typically will want to know that the seller is at least not aware of, and has not received notice of, any violations.

The buyer may also want some assurance that the seller is not aware that it has violated any laws relating to equal employment opportunities, hiring, or other laws affecting employment and employment practices.

These compliance matters may be the subject of specific provisions in the indemnification section of the agreement. Even if it is not possible for the seller to give absolute assurance of compliance in certain areas, buyer's often request that the seller retain responsibility for pre-closing noncompliance. This allocation of risk and responsibility is one of the major negotiating points in any US acquisition.

Chapter 34: Employment Issues in Context of Acquisitions

Employment Protection

Unlike many non-US jurisdictions, there are no US statutes requiring that employees be retained or given specific severance pay upon termination of employment in an acquisition, although (Labour and Employment – Special Problems and Statutes Related to Mass Layoffs and Terminations), federal law (e.g., the "WARN"Act) and some similar state laws require advance notice if an entire plant is to be closed or a certain percentage of employees are to be terminated.

Employees have no statutory right to review, approve, or even be consulted about an acquisition of their employer. Employees do not automatically become the employees of the acquiring corporation in an asset purchase, although they will remain employees of the target or successor in a share acquisition or merger.

Nevertheless, a non-US buyer should not assume that it has an entirely free hand in dealing with employees. Most US employers have adopted employment policies that may legally bind successors. These will often provide for some form of termination compensation or severance, unless the employees are offered employment with substantially the same salary and, perhaps, benefits by the acquiring corporation.

For this and other reasons, the seller will often insist that the buyer agree to employ its existing workforce and may want to specify the terms and conditions of that employment. As with other economic issues, these matters will be negotiated between the buyer and seller.

Related matters, such as accrued vacation pay, likely will have to be dealt with as well, since the employees will expect to retain these accrued benefits after closing. A non-US buyer especially will not want to appear to be insensitive to employee expectations.

Labour Agreements

In a stock purchase or merger, the buyer is bound by any collective bargaining (i.e., labour) agreement to which the target corporation is a party. A buyer will be bound in an asset acquisition only if it expressly assumes the collective bargaining agreement. A buyer will usually want to take advantage of the comparatively weak bargaining position of the target's workforce to renegotiate the terms of employment. Consequently, it will generally resist assuming any collective bargaining agreements.

The buyer will, however, be required to recognize any existing labour union and bargain with it in good faith. Many non-US buyers will find US labour unions easier to deal with than their non-US counterparts. A collective bargaining agreement will bind only one company and its employees, not an entire industry.

Termination Notice

The federal government and some state governments, as well as many collective bargaining agreements, require advance notice when certain employment sites are closed.

Depending on the degree of continuity in an acquisition, such statutes or contract provisions may apply to the buyer. Federal law also requires that a terminated employee be allowed to continue any employer-sponsored health program for a period of time but at the cost of the employee. Certain states, such as Massachusetts, may impose this cost on the employer.

Pensions and Other Benefits

If the target has maintained any employee benefit programs, including pension plans, responsibility for continued adequate funding of these obligations may pass to the buyer, even in an asset acquisition. These plans are subject to extensive federal regulation. A buyer of a business may incur significant obligations created prior to the acquisition, including making up any under-funding of the pension plan. In an asset acquisition, the seller would generally want the buyer to continue its existing pension plans, since termination of a plan can be expensive and time consuming.

Termination is avoidable only if the buyer is willing to have a plan that is comparable in scope, although not necessarily identical, to the seller's existing plan. In any acquisition, the target corporation's pension plan should be examined in detail by experts (lawyers and actuaries) hired by the buyer, to avoid having the buyer incur substantial unexpected liabilities.

Chapter 35: Material Assets

Physical Facilities

The buyer typically wants to obtain clear title to any plants or other real estate owned by the target, since these are material to the operation of the business. Title to real estate is transferred by a deed, which is publicly recorded. (Title certificates are also used in certain locations.)

There is no notary of the kind found in many civil law countries. In most US states, title to real property is investigated and assured by title insurance companies. The title company will insure clear title, subject to certain specified exceptions, such as identified mortgages, easements, and servitudes.

If significant real estate is owned by the target, title insurance is often obtained even if shares are being acquired and no real property is actually being transferred.

The buyer may also obtain a survey of the property that indicates the location of all buildings, easements, servitudes (such as utility lines), and other matters affecting the physical layout of the property, and that discloses any difficulty with access to the property. As noted above, the buyer may wish to obtain an environmental audit as well. The buyer will want to ensure that the property is being used legally and in compliance with all building codes and zoning ordinances; these will be covered by title insurance only if specifically requested and paid for.

In an asset acquisition, the transfer of real estate will require the payment of state and local transfer taxes, but with certain exceptions, these tend to be far lower than in most other countries.

Intellectual Property

In many businesses, intellectual property constitutes a substantial component of value. In that case, the buyer typically conducts a thorough investigation of title to all intellectual property, including trademarks and patents, and ensures that title to such property can be effectively transferred to it in the case of an asset acquisition.

A non-US buyer may be particularly interested in the extent of foreign protection of the acquired intellectual property. The buyer likely will also want assurance that all necessary consents to the assignment of any intellectual property licenses have been obtained. This may be necessary even in the case of certain stock acquisitions if the license is terminable upon a material change in control of the target enterprise.

A major issue often encountered with non-US buyers is the seller's unwillingness to warrant that its patents are valid, since such a warranty goes far beyond a mere representation of good title. A significant number of challenged patents are ruled invalid in the United States, and so a warranty of validity will generally be resisted by US sellers.

Agreements and Licenses

Agreements and licenses that are material to the success of a business may be jeopardized by an acquisition. For example, following the foreign acquisition of Firestone, General

Motors announced that it would no longer purchase tires from Firestone as original equipment on its automobiles.

An acquisition agreement typically will require disclosure of any contract above a certain size or extending beyond certain duration, to alert the buyer of the commitments to which the business is subject and advise the buyer of the consents that must be obtained to assume such agreements or leases. The other party to such contracts or leases may be reluctant to consent to assignment without compensation if, for example, the rent or other compensation is below market. Thus, the acquisition agreement may contain additional representations regarding assignability and a lack of knowledge by the seller that any material business will be lost solely as a result of the acquisition.

Chapter 36: Liabilities

Product Liability

A principal concern of any buyer of a US business is strict liability for personal injuries resulting from products manufactured and sold by the business. As in most other countries, the manufacturer or seller of a product in the United States is liable for damages sustained as a result of the manufacturer's or seller's negligence.

However, under the US doctrine of strict liability, one who sells a product is liable for any physical harm caused to the ultimate user or consumer or to its property, if the product at the time of sale is in a defective condition (such that it is unreasonably dangerous to the user); the seller is engaged in the business of selling the product; and the product may be expected to and does reach the user without substantial change.

Combined with the propensity of US juries to award substantial damages, the doctrine of strict liability makes product claims a material cost of doing business in the United States.

Accordingly, buyers often want some assurance from the seller that such exposure will not be unreasonable in amount. The buyer also may want to investigate the historical experience of the seller to ascertain whether the business itself involves undue risks.

In a stock purchase or a merger (or in an asset acquisition in some states), the buyer is often concerned about assuming responsibility for products sold prior to the closing.

Although the seller may represent that it knows of no such liabilities, there is generally no way the seller can give complete assurance in this regard. Therefore, the parties often allocate responsibility as part of the indemnification provisions.

Typically, sellers remain responsible for any products sold or shipped (and sometimes manufactured) prior to the closing and buyers are responsible for products sold or shipped after the closing.

Indemnification for product liability will often be either unlimited in time or limited to the applicable state's statute of limitations. This latter limitation is not very meaningful since it generally begins to run only at the time the person is injured, which may be long after the product is sold or shipped.

Tax Liabilities

In an asset acquisition, the buyer will almost never become directly liable for income and most other taxes based on the operation of the business prior to the closing. However, certain ad valorem taxes (those based on the value of property) may constitute a lien on the assets purchased. In addition, the failure to conduct thorough due diligence and/or comply with certain procedures could result in the buyer assuming liability for state or local sales or use taxes owed by the seller.

In this case, it is normal for the seller to accept complete responsibility for tax liabilities attributable to the operation of the business prior to the closing and indemnify the buyer against any such liabilities. Such indemnification generally runs for the period of the statute of limitations.

Other Liabilities

In the United States, the seller often will represent that there are no undisclosed liabilities of the business, contingent or otherwise. If the target has any undisclosed liabilities, they will usually be the responsibility of the seller pursuant to an indemnification. In an asset acquisition, the buyer often will expressly not assume any liabilities other than those specifically identified in the agreement.

No Material Change

The seller often will represent that there has been no material adverse change in the operations or financial condition of the business since the date of the most recent financial statements or some other cut-off date. In addition, lack of any material adverse change will often be a condition of closing. A typical provision in an acquisition agreement will limit the seller's right to conduct the business between contract signing and closing other than in accordance with past practice and in the ordinary course of business and will prohibit the seller from making any material change in the business, making any major purchases or investments, incurring any significant obligations or liabilities, or changing compensation or other employee benefits without the consent of the buyer.

Chapter 37: Other Legal Matters

There are a number of other legal matters that may be of concern in an acquisition, as discussed below.

Distributors and Agents

Acquisition agreements often require disclosure of all material distribution and sales representative agreements and arrangements. Unlike the practice in many other countries, in most states the buyer is free to terminate distributors and sales representatives without being liable for mandatory termination compensation payments. Few states have statutes requiring such compensation. However, there is a general trend in the United States against arbitrary or abusive terminations.

Thus, a buyer may seek to document that any such terminations are made pursuant to a reorganization of the acquired business's distribution arrangements. A buyer may also seek to ensure that such terminations are not motivated by matters constituting antitrust violations. For example, it would be illegal to terminate a price-cutting distributor in an attempt to control pricing.

Immigration

A non-US acquirer will often contemplate sending executives and skilled technical experts to assist with the operation of the business after the closing. Those individuals who wish to enter the United States to attend meetings or similar activities may use either the B-1 Business Visitor visa status or Visa Waiver status, if available to visit the United States. In the case of a transferring executive, skilled technical expert, or other employee who will provide direct service to the acquired company in the United States, it is necessary to obtain an appropriate visa that authorizes employment in advance of the assignment. Since obtaining visas may be somewhat time consuming, any important personnel transfers should be planned with the help of experts well in advance of the closing.

Importation of Parts and Components

All matters pertaining to the importation of merchandise into the United States fall within the exclusive jurisdiction of the federal government. Many products imported into the United States are subject to the payment of import duties, generally payable on an ad valorem basis and determined by their specific classification.

The Bureau of Customs and Border Protection has the right to challenge any claimed valuation, particularly where the transaction is between a non-US parent and a US subsidiary. If a non-US buyer plans to use an acquired corporation, for example, to assemble parts and components imported from abroad, it will want to ascertain early on that it will be able to import the parts and components without being subject to quotas (quotas are quite rare) and obtain some guidance as to the import duty cost of such importations into the United States.

There are a number of special forms of customs entry, such as foreign trade zones, that may be of particular interest to a non-US buyer.

Products of non-US origin may be shipped to a foreign trade zone located in the United States without making a formal customs entry or paying any US customs duties. Such products may be stored, sold for export, or assembled while located within the zone and then re-exported, all without incurring any US customs duty.

A non-US buyer may encounter additional costs on imports to the United States, such as antidumping and countervailing duties. These are imposed when products are imported at what the US government considers an unjustifiably low price.

In some cases, restrictions such as quotas may be imposed on certain products. If the acquired business will be dependent on imported materials or components, the non-US buyer should review its plans and anticipated pricing with customs counsel prior to proceeding with an acquisition.

Organizing the Acquisition Vehicle

Whatever the form of the acquisition, it is likely that the buyer will want to organize a US limited liability company or corporation to act as the acquisition vehicle. (Some investors may prefer a form of partnership because of the tax or other advantages available in their own country.) The acquisition vehicle will be organized before the closing and probably prior to signing the acquisition agreement.

Alternatively, the acquisition agreement may be signed by the buyer and assigned to the acquisition vehicle prior to the closing.

144

Chapter 38: Closing U.S. Acquisition

The closing of a US acquisition will be organized primarily by legal counsel for the buyer and seller.

Transfer Documents

The transfer documents to be executed and delivered at the closing will depend on the nature of the transaction. In a purchase of shares, or LLC membership interests represented by certificates, the seller typically will deliver certificates representing all of the shares or membership interests in the target corporation either endorsed to the buyer or accompanied by an executed "stock power" (or power of attorney) authorizing the transfer of the shares or membership interests on the books of the target. Membership interests not represented by certificates will be transferred by a form of assignment.

In a merger, the parties will execute a formal plan of merger (in most states) for filing with the secretaries of state of the jurisdictions in which the respective corporations or limited liability companies are organized. This document may be considerably shorter than the definitive merger agreement and may have to be notarized. These formalities will be accomplished immediately prior to the closing and the plan of merger may be sent ahead to the appropriate state agencies to be ready for filing on the date of the closing.

An asset acquisition generally is more complicated. Real estate will be transferred by deeds for each parcel. Deeds typically will have to be notarized and recorded in the locality in which the real estate is located. Recording will be completed on the date of the closing or shortly thereafter. At the closing, the title insurance company will execute and deliver a binding commitment insuring title to the real estate.

Personal property will be transferred by bill of sale, which requires no formalities. Agreements and other intangibles will be transferred by a form of assignment, which may be combined with the bill of sale. Separate assignment documents may be required for patents and certain other assets, some of which are subject to formal requirements.

Payment

In an international acquisition, payment is more often effected by wire transfer than cashier's check. The disadvantage of a cashier's check is that it will have to be deposited for collection, and so, funds may not be available to the seller on the day of closing. This can cause the loss of a substantial amount of interest. Wire transfers make funds immediately available once the transfer is acknowledged by the seller's bank, but delays sometimes occur. International wire transfers are more likely to be delayed on a Monday or Friday because of the large volume of other transfers and transactions on those days. Therefore, whenever possible, it is preferable to close in the middle of the week. If the closing must be held at the beginning or end of the week or timing is crucial, payment may be made by a federal funds cashier's check which is somewhat inconvenient for the buyer to obtain but which provides immediately available funds to the seller.

Other Agreements

A number of ancillary agreements may be executed at the closing. These are likely to include the following.

Non-competition Agreements

There are business and tax reasons why the buyer often wants key seller personnel to agree not to compete with the target business for some period of time after the closing. Such agreements are generally enforceable if they are reasonable in scope and duration and designed to preserve the benefit of the acquisition to the buyer.

Employment Agreements

It is not unusual for the seller of a privately held business, and possibly family members, to have been employed by the corporation prior to the acquisition. A significant consideration in agreeing to sell the business may be some assurance of continuity of employment. In acquisitions of professionally managed entities, the buyer often wants to ensure that certain key individuals will be available to operate the target business after the closing. This is most often true of top executives and important technical personnel.

In these cases, either the buyer or seller may require that employment agreements be executed with such key persons at or prior to the closing.

Leases and Licenses

It may not be possible to transfer all of the tangible and intangible property necessary to operate the target business to the buyer. For example, the seller may continue to use key software or technology in its retained businesses. In such cases, tangible property may have to be leased and intangible property licensed to the target business.

Service Agreements

If the buyer is purchasing a portion of an integrated business, the buyer may not receive a fully stand-alone operation. In this case, the seller may have to provide post-closing services to the buyer on a short-term or, occasionally, long-term basis.

Computer access is a common example of such a post-closing service provided by the seller.

Other Documents

A number of other documents may also be delivered at the closing. These include legal opinions from counsel for both parties. It is normal to deliver a certified copy of the certificate or articles of incorporation or association of the target company to the buyer as well as a certificate issued by the appropriate secretary of state indicating that the target company is in "good standing" in its state of incorporation.

It is also customary for the target (and for the buyer) to deliver a certificate affirming that all representations and warranties in the acquisition agreement are true and correct as of the day of closing. Unless they are to continue on in such capacities, the officers and directors of the target in a stock acquisition and the managers of a limited liability company will deliver written resignations. This is not necessary in an asset acquisition, since employees are not automatically transferred with the business.

Chapter 39: Post-Acquisition Trade (Import/Export) Issues

Once an acquisition is complete, the buyer needs to be aware of a few potential import-and export-control compliance details that can significantly impact the business' operations if they are mishandled.

First, (Direct Sales), the business needs (among other things) a customs bond if it is importing. If a new entity was created which bought assets in the acquisition, then that new entity will need a customs bond in its name.

If the acquisition is one of shares, a new customs bond may not be needed. If the acquired business remains and continues to operate under the same name, its pre-existing customs bond can simply be maintained. However, it is common in a share-purchase acquisition for there to be an official name change of the acquired company, and in such a case the business must officially change its importer-of-record name with the Bureau of Customs and Border Protection and have the name change reflected in its customs bond by either executing a bond rider or obtaining an entirely new bond in the new company name.

Second, if the business exports goods under licenses from the US Departments of State, Commerce, and/or Treasury, these licenses may need to be assigned or transferred in accordance with applicable regulations or altogether new licenses may need to be obtained in the name of the new entity.

Finally, both the US Departments of State and Commerce follow a rule that an export is deemed to have occurred when certain foreign nationals, when present in the United States, are exposed to information related to an item the export of which is controlled. These are so-called "deemed exports." If a license would be needed to export that information to the home country of the foreign national, then a license is needed for the deemed export to legally occur.

This can become an issue for a foreign buyer, because it is likely that the buyer will dispatch certain of its employees to the acquired business in the United States to assist with post-acquisition integration. If the operations of the business concern items which require licenses when exported, it may be necessary to acquire licenses for deemed exports of information related to these controlled items to the foreign-national employees of the buyer.

Chapter 40: Business Entities

The previous chapters highlight how a non-US buyer often will establish a US acquisition vehicle in the form of a partnership or corporation to acquire a US target. Establishing a formal presence in the United States, either through acquisition of an existing business or through formation of a branch, joint venture or subsidiary generally involves a greater level of commitment than selling directly in the United States through sales representatives or distributors.

The next few chapters, therefore, provides an overview of the various types of business entities through which a US presence may be established. In particular, this focuses upon three limited liability entities:

- Corporations
- Limited liability companies
- Limited partnerships.

We highlight several factors, including issues of taxation that typically influence the decision of which form of US business entity is the appropriate vehicle to use to establish a US presence. We will also addressing the formation of a branch, subsidiary and joint venture in later chapters of this book.

Formation of Corporations

The sole form of share-company in the United States is the corporation. US corporate law has few mandatory provisions and is without restriction on the number of stockholders (except in the case of a close corporation) and with free transferability of shares. This flexibility facilitates structuring a corporation to fit the needs and objectives of a foreign investor.

Place of Incorporation

The US has no national (federal) company law, and regulation of the formation and operation of corporations is left largely to the individual states.

Unlike a widespread European practice that requires a company be formed under the law of the jurisdiction in which its principal place of business is located, a US corporation may be formed under the laws of any state and have its principal place of business elsewhere so long as it "qualifies to do business" in each state in which it operates. This means that investors may choose the state law that best fits their needs.

Delaware law is particularly well suited to operation without in-person meetings (i.e., meetings by teleconference) or even without meetings at all (i.e., by written consent), a factor that can be quite convenient where stockholders and directors outside the United States are involved. In addition, the Delaware annual reporting requirements are simple and Delaware law and practice are well-adapted to corporations whose principal place of business is not located in Delaware.

Delaware courts are also well-versed in corporate matters. On the other hand, a Delaware corporation doing business in another state may have to pay two annual franchise fees. This factor may be sufficient reason to incorporate under the law of the state in which the corporation will be doing business. Because of the pre-eminence of Delaware, any references to legal rules in this chapter are to those of Delaware unless otherwise indicated.

In general, state laws do not restrict the citizenship or residency of officers, directors or stockholders of a corporation, and so the choice of place of incorporation is unlikely to be critical to a foreign investor. With a few exceptions, a corporation may be reorganized under the laws of another state at any time without substantial tax liability, although this can be rather expensive to implement.

Formalities

Generally, a corporation is formed when its certificate of incorporation (or, in certain states, articles of incorporation) is filed with the Secretary of State of the state in which it is to be incorporated. The certificate of incorporation may be executed by anyone acting as incorporator, and thus need not be executed by an employee of the non-US investor. No special formalities, such as notarization, are required. Thus, a US corporation could be formed on a few days, and even a few hours, notice.

Name

In most states, the name of the corporation must provide indicia of corporate status e.g., "Corporation," "Incorporated," "Limited," "Company" or an abbreviation thereof.

The name also must be distinguishable from other existing or reserved entity names. For most states, one may determine by telephone or on the Secretary of State's website if a particular name is available. Since corporate laws operate only at the state level, a name could be available in one state, but blocked in many others. On the other hand, unlike in some non-US jurisdictions, almost any name can be used (that is, it need not be descriptive of the business or be that of a stockholder). Finally, the name may be reserved for a limited period of time in anticipation of filing the certificate of incorporation.

Purpose

The purpose of the company may be stated very broadly, including "any activity permitted by law." However, in some states there must nonetheless be some indication of the business in which the company will actually engage. This purpose may be expanded in the future by means of an amendment to the certificate of incorporation.

Procedures

The principal steps in organizing a Delaware corporation are the following:

- The certificate of incorporation is executed by an "incorporator" and filed with the Secretary of State of the State of Delaware.

  The incorporator may be a natural person, partnership, association or corporation and need not be a resident of or domiciled in Delaware.

  The incorporator may act alone or with others and most US jurisdictions require only one incorporator. In practice, the incorporator is usually an individual; sometimes a lawyer, paralegal or law clerk, or an employee of a corporate services company who, for a fee, will provide incorporating services. (The certificate of incorporation must also list a registered agent and registered office in the state for purposes of accepting service of process in the context of litigation and a corporate service company is often retained for this purpose when the corporation's principle place of business is outside of Delaware.)

- The investor-stockholders subscribe for the number of shares that are to be issued by the corporation and pay in their capital contribution. This may be done before the filing of the certificate of incorporation. There is no minimum capital requirement.

- The initial board of directors (the members of which may be named in the certificate of incorporation or appointed by the incorporator) then holds the initial or organizational meeting (or all execute written resolutions) at which (or by which) the board typically:

(i) Approves the certificate of incorporation and the actions of the incorporator.

(ii) Adopts bylaws for the company. The bylaws generally govern the organization and operation of a corporation. The bylaws of a privately held corporation remain a private document (that is, they are not filed with a state Secretary of State). Unless otherwise provided in the certificate of incorporation, the bylaws may be amended only by stockholders entitled to vote. Bylaws for corporations formed in other states would be similar in most respects.

(iii) Appoints the officers of the corporation.

(iv) Authorizes officers to qualify the corporation to do business in whatever other state may be necessary because of the nature of the corporation's activities in that state.

(v) Adopts a fiscal year, corporate seal and form of stock certificate.

(vi) Approves opening a bank account.

(vii) Accepts subscriptions for the corporation's shares.

(viii) Appoints independent auditors, if any. US law does not require non-public companies to appoint auditors, although a corporation's banks and principal creditors will usually require financial statements certified by independent auditors.

(ix) Approves any agreement among the stockholders. Such approval is not mandatory, however.

- A federal employer identification number is obtained from the Internal Revenue Service, or IRS, and a bank account is opened in the name of the corporation. At this point, the corporation is able to engage in any lawful business within its purpose.

If the corporation is organized under the laws of any other state, the steps to be followed would be substantially similar to those outlined above for a Delaware corporation. Although some states impose relatively small minimum capital requirements that must be paid in before the corporation may commence business, in Delaware and many other states, the corporation may commence operation even without capital or stockholder subscriptions. Nevertheless, operating with grossly inadequate capital is one of several factors that courts consider in determining whether to "pierce the corporate veil" and hold the stockholders liable for the obligations of the corporation in certain circumstances.

Chapter 41: Corporation Shares and Capital

1. Common and Preferred Shares

The ordinary shares issued by US corporations are generally referred to as "common shares" or stock. It is also possible for a corporation to issue preferred shares, that is, shares carrying a priority with respect to dividends, distribution of capital upon liquidation, or both.

Preferred shares may be redeemed by the company under specific conditions at a fixed price or at a price determined in accordance with a pre-established formula. Although preferred dividends are normally payable only out of profits, and only to the extent there are profits, such dividends may be made cumulative; thus the dividend payable in a year when the company had no profits available would continue as an obligation to be repaid in later, profitable years before any dividends could be paid on common shares.

The use of both common and preferred shares in various combinations, often in conjunction with stockholder loans, offers considerable flexibility to investors in financing a US subsidiary.

2. Authorized Shares

Stockholders need not subscribe for all of the shares that a corporation is authorized by its certificate to issue, and it is often true that a corporation will have substantially more shares authorized than issued. In general, the board of directors may cause the corporation to issue additional shares

159

up to the maximum authorized by the certificate of incorporation, but an amendment to the certificate of incorporation is required to increase the amount of authorized shares, thus necessitating a vote by both the board of directors and the stockholders.

3. Treasury Shares

A US corporation may purchase its own shares, subject to certain limitations. Such treasury shares may not be voted and may not receive dividends, but the corporation may dispose of them in the same manner as any of its other property subject to federal and state securities laws.

4. Par and No-Par Shares; Absence of Bearer Shares

A corporation generally may issue shares with or without par value. No-par shares offer certain flexibility, but if the corporation will be issuing a large number of shares, shares with a nominal par value (e.g., $.01 or $.001) may carry a lower annual franchise tax rate. Many foreign investors opt for shares with par value out of a sense of familiarity. Bearer shares are not permitted in the United States, and so ownership of all shares in an US corporation is registered on the internal books of the corporation. The identity of the stockholders normally need not be disclosed in any public document.

5. Non-Voting Stock

Delaware and other US corporations may issue one or more classes of shares which may have limited or no voting rights.

When shares do have voting rights, voting power need not be in proportion to capital contribution or economic interest.

6.   Capital and Surplus

The concept of capital in US corporate law is both more flexible and less important than under many other legal systems. The emphasis in the United States tends to be on promoting the growth of the corporation rather than preserving its capital, and ultimately, the amount of capital often bears little relationship to a company's actual importance.

In the United States, persons dealing with a corporation often rely upon its net worth (as indicated by its balance sheet), its earnings (as indicated on its income statement) or some other representative measure of value, rather than upon its stated capital. As a result, the directors of a corporation are less likely to be held liable for a failure to preserve the corporation's capital than in, for example, Europe.

If shares are issued in excess of par value (or at an aggregate price in excess of stated capital in the case of no-par shares), that surplus is called paid-in surplus.

It is customary that only a portion of the contributions of stockholders to the corporation be allocated to capital and the balance treated as paid-in surplus.

In many states, this would permit dividends to be paid out of these contributions, which can add flexibility to the financial operations of the corporation.

7. Cash, Property and Services as Capital Contributions

Shares may be issued for cash, personal or real property, a promissory note or services already performed. Shares with par value may not be issued for less than par value. Shares may not be issued for services to be performed in the future.

No public appraisal or court approval of property contributed for shares is required; the valuation of non-cash contributions by the board of directors is conclusive in the absence of actual fraud under most states' laws.

8. Limitations upon the Transfer of Shares

US corporate law imposes few restrictions on the transfer of shares. In closely held corporations with more than one stockholder, there are practical motivations to restrict the transfer of shares. Agreements among stockholders restricting transferability are enforceable, and can provide for the following type of restrictions:

Transfer Subject to Stockholder (or Board of Directors) Consent Under the laws of certain states, a requirement that shares may be transferred only with the consent of a specified percentage of stockholders or directors is permissible, subject, however, to a requirement that this power be exercised in good faith.

However, the laws of many other states do not expressly provide for such restrictions, and it is possible that the provision would be denied enforcement if it were deemed to be equivalent to an absolute prohibition on transfer, a prohibition considered to be contrary to public policy. Again, good faith is required for enforcement of such a provision.

Prohibitions on Transfer to Particular Persons or Classes

It is possible under Delaware law and the laws of a number of other states to prohibit transfers to designated persons or classes of persons, such as competitors.

Right of First Offer or First Refusal

It is possible (and customary) to provide for a right of "first offer" or "first refusal," that is, a right given to the corporation or the other stockholders to purchase the shares of a stockholder who wishes to dispose of some or all of his shares, either at a price fixed in advance of offering the shares to an outside purchaser or at the price and terms offered by an outside purchaser usually up to an amount to maintain a stockholder's existing percentage ownership. While such restrictions are acceptable generally in the United States, they may have the effect of diminishing the liquidity of the shares, especially if the provision is not drafted with great care.

Pre-emptive Rights

Existing stockholders have no automatic and initial right to receive a proportionate share of newly issues stock. However, in contrast to certain states wherein a preemptive right is a default provision, a preemptive right may be included in the certificate of incorporation for a new corporation.

Notice of Restriction

The foregoing restrictions on transfer may be accomplished by inclusion of a provision in the certificate of incorporation or bylaws of the corporation. More often, a provision is included in a private agreement among the stockholders. Regardless of where the restriction appears, a notation, or "legend," indicating the existence of a restriction on share transfers must be placed on the reverse side of the stock certificate in order to be sure that the restriction is binding on third parties.

The absence of a commercial register in the United States means that there is no other means of effectively notifying third parties of such restrictions.

Chapter 42: Corporate Structure

A corporation consists of three principal constituencies; the stockholders, the board of directors and the officers. The functions of each, which differ from those in many other legal systems, are as follows:

Stockholders

The stockholders are the owners of the corporation. In US corporations, except for a limited number of regulated industries, such as banking and insurance in certain states, have no restriction as to the nationality or place of residence of stockholders. A corporation may have a single stockholder both upon formation and thereafter without creating any special risk that the stockholder would be liable for the obligations of the corporation.

The stockholders generally have the following powers:

1. Election of Directors/Cumulative Voting

In most states, a simple majority of the stockholders may elect the entire board of directors. However, the certificate of incorporation may provide for cumulative voting, whereby stockholders may elect directors in proportion to their shareholding in the company.

As a result of cumulative voting, a substantial minority stockholder could elect one or more directors. However, if it is desired that minority stockholders be guaranteed the right to elect a fixed number of directors, this should be accomplished by an agreement among the stockholders.

2. Merger, Sale of Assets, and Dissolution

In general, a merger, sale of all or substantially all of the assets, or dissolution of the company must be approved by stockholders entitled to vote and owning a majority of the outstanding shares of the company. The certificate of incorporation or the laws of certain states, however, may require the approval of an extraordinary majority, or supermajority, of stockholders.

3. Amendment of Certificate of Incorporation and Bylaws

The stockholders may amend the certificate of incorporation by simple majority vote unless otherwise specified in the certificate of incorporation or provided by agreement among the stockholders. In certain states, the amendment must receive the approval of a supermajority of stockholders. In addition, in most states the stockholders may amend the bylaws by a simple majority, although many states allow this power to be given to the board of directors concurrently by inclusion of a provision to that effect in the certificate of incorporation or bylaws. However, Delaware recently amended its corporate law statute to provide that a by-law adopted by shareholders that sets the vote required for director elections may not be further amended or repealed by the board of directors.

4. Declaration of Dividends

The stockholders do not have the right to declare dividends. As explained below, this power is reserved to the board of directors in a US corporation.

5. Stockholder Meetings

The stockholders may, to some extent, restrict the powers of the board of directors by requiring stockholder approval for certain decisions. The stockholders must formally exercise their powers at meetings of the stockholders.

The stockholders must meet at least annually on a date and at a time fixed by the bylaws unless they act by written consent as described below. Stockholders may hold special meetings at anytime.

The following are some of the principal procedural aspects of a stockholder meeting:

Notice and Waiver

Notice of a meeting must be given in accordance with the bylaws but generally under state law must neither be less than 10 nor more than 60 days prior to the date of the meeting.

However, these temporal requirements may be altered by the dictates of the federal securities laws.

A stockholder may waive notice formally in writing or impliedly by attendance at a meeting (except if attendance is for the purpose of protesting lack of notice).

Quorum

In most states, a majority of the shares entitled to vote constitutes a quorum so long as the action to be taken at the meeting does not require a greater percentage vote. In Delaware, the certificate of incorporation or bylaws may specify a quorum of as low as one third of the shares entitled to vote.

Proxy

Stockholders may vote through proxies, and the presence of a proxy holder at a meeting will count towards constituting a quorum. Proxies are generally revocable and are automatically revoked if a new proxy is given.

Action by Written Consent of Stockholders

In lieu of a formal meeting, the stockholders may act through consent in writing executed, in most states, by the stockholders holding the requisite voting power necessary to authorize the particular action. Consent resolutions are a considerable convenience where a wholly-owned subsidiary is involved since they avoid the charade of holding a "meeting" of the sole stockholder.

Chapter 43: Board of Directors

A US corporation is generally managed by its board of directors, which has the power to carry out substantially all corporate acts not specifically reserved to the stockholders. US corporations have only one board of directors, unlike the dual board of directors arrangement in certain European entities, for example, a German Aktiengesellschaft.

Although most states allow a board of directors to be comprised of only one director, typically a board of directors will have more than one director, with three or five being the number of directors most commonly specified. Only individuals may act as directors. There is no general requirement that directors be citizens or residents of the United States or of the state of incorporation.

Certain states do impose residency or citizenship requirements on directors of companies operating in certain sectors of the economy, such as insurance and banking, and federal law limits foreign participation in a few industries that are deemed particularly sensitive (e.g., defence, commercial fishing, communications and the like). Directors do not have to be stockholders and therefore do not require qualifying shares.

As noted, the board of directors exercises all corporate powers not reserved to the stockholders.

Those powers include:
Management

The directors as a group manage the corporation. The board of directors sets policy for the corporation and is responsible for its performance. It will specifically authorize significant transactions, but the actual day-to-day operations are usually delegated to the officers, with the board supervising the conduct of the officers.

Dividends

Unlike the European model, for example, the directors of a US corporation have the power to declare dividends without the participation of the stockholders.

Merger, Consolidation, Dissolution

The board of directors will normally recommend the merger, consolidation or dissolution of the corporation to the stockholders.

Board of Directors Meetings

Normally, directors do not represent the corporation in its dealings with third parties; this is typically done by the officers. Rather, the directors, in principle, act as a body through meetings called in accordance with the bylaws.

Directors must personally participate in meetings though they may also do so through telephone conference. Resolutions generally are adopted by a simple majority of the directors present and voting at a meeting at which a quorum is present.

The following are some of the principal procedural aspects of a meeting of the board of directors are:

Notice and Waiver

Notice requirements for meetings may be very short, perhaps 24 hours, although foreign investors typically require longer periods if directors are located on two continents. Modern US law is extremely flexible in this regard, however, and notice may be formally waived in writing at any time by a director or impliedly waived by his or her presence at a meeting.

Quorum

A majority of the directors will constitute a quorum unless a different number is specified in the certificate of incorporation or bylaws. Most states allow a quorum of no less than one third of the directors.

Proxy

Directors of a corporation may not vote by proxy, the rationale being that the corporation must benefit from the unique skills and judgment of a particular director when deciding an issue.

Action by Written Consent of Directors

Directors may also act through a written consent in writing signed by every director. Thus, a formal meeting of the directors need never be held, even in connection with the organization of the company. This proves to be a considerable convenience for foreign investors.

Officers

The board of directors normally delegates responsibility for the day-to-day operations of a corporation to the officers. Because there is no commercial register in the United States, third parties rely upon an officer's apparent authority based on his or her title, that is, they rely upon the officer enjoying the authority normally attendant to such title. Thus, titles should be chosen with care. Officers are not normally given powers of attorney and a person dealing with the corporation ordinarily should not expect one.

The officers generally consist of a chief executive officer, who may also hold the title of "chairman of the board of directors" or, more often, "president," one or more vice presidents, a secretary and a chief financial offer.

The board of directors appoints the officers and may remove them at any time. At a minimum, the corporation should have a chief executive officer and a secretary. One person may hold more than one office; however, it is recommended, but not required, that different individuals hold the offices of president and secretary. The authority and functions of each of these officers are set forth in detail in the bylaws.

The typical functions of the various corporate officers may be summarized as follows:

Chief Executive Officer

The chief executive officer has the power to act on behalf of the corporation and represent it in the ordinary course of business. Moreover, he or she supervises the administration and operation of the corporation's business. Where the US

Corporation is a subsidiary of a foreign parent, it may be advisable to have a representative of the foreign parent who is resident in the United States serve as chief executive officer if at all possible. Neither the chief executive officer nor any other officer will be able to act alone on matters other than matters in the ordinary course of the corporation's business without specific authorization from the board of directors, which authorization will have to be certified by the secretary of the corporation in some instances, as described below.

Some corporations also provide for a chief operating officer who deals with the daily operations of the corporation under the direction of the chief executive officer.

Vice President

The vice president acts in the absence or at the request of the chief executive officer and exercises such other powers as may be delegated by the board of directors. If there is more than one vice president, one among them is often designated the executive vice president, or senior vice president. Very large corporations and banks may have a hierarchy of vice presidents.

Where the US Corporation is a subsidiary of a foreign parent and where the president or chief executive officer will not reside in the United States, it may be advisable to appoint the local manager as a vice president. There are many circumstances in which persons having business with the US Corporation will expect to deal with an officer of the company and it will prove useful to have someone available for that purpose.

Secretary

The secretary is a position unfamiliar to many practitioners in civil law countries.

The secretary is the officer of the corporation responsible for maintaining certain books and records of the company, especially the minutes of the board of directors meeting and the share transfer records.

Furthermore, it is common in the United States to require that the secretary of a company attest to the authority of an officer to execute any important documents, particularly bank documents. This is so because there is no equivalent to the commercial register in which the names of persons having signature powers for the corporation may be listed.

Accordingly, because outsiders cannot independently verify an officer's authority to represent and sign for the corporation, they often require the participation of two officers (of which one often is the secretary) in substantial transactions. In this role, the secretary does not truly represent the company, but rather merely attests to the fact that the officer who does act on behalf of the company is authorized to do so, either under the company's bylaws or by a specific resolution of the board of directors. Ultimately, the secretary safeguards against an officer exceeding his or her authority when acting on behalf of the company.

An in-house or outside attorney may fill this role for his or her clients, which may be particularly helpful for foreign investors. The board of directors may also elect an assistant secretary to act in the absence of the secretary. Since there is no way to verify who is the secretary, the process can be circular in its logic; thus an outside attorney is sometimes selected as secretary or assistant secretary to add credibility to the attestation.

Chief Financial Officer

The chief financial officer is responsible for supervising the financial affairs of the company and the management of its funds. In a large company, he or she may be aided in his role by the controller. The controller has a function somewhat equivalent to that of an internal auditor, but in the United States the controller's function is not required or defined by law. Thus, the controller does not act independently of the company's management. In general, US company law does not impose the kind of independent financial control for the protection of stockholders imposed by many European company laws, and there is no position in a corporation equivalent to the auditor or commissar found in many European companies.

Nevertheless, the Securities and Exchange Commission, or SEC, in the case of public companies, or the corporation's bank, in the case of private companies, typically requires an annual audit (which is more than a review or compilation under US generally accepted accounting principles) of the corporation's books and records by an independent certified public accountant.

The Sarbanes-Oxley Act also requires that the chief financial officer and chief executive officer of companies with securities that are listed traded or otherwise registered in the United States to certify as to the corporation's internal control over financial reporting.

Chapter 44: Corporate Governance

Liability of Stockholders

Businesses are conducted in corporate form primarily in order to enjoy the benefit of limited liability. The investment that a stockholder makes in a corporation is necessarily at risk but the stockholder typically is not responsible for the liabilities or losses of the corporation beyond that investment. Nonetheless, if the separate existence of the corporation is not respected, there is a risk that creditors will be able to disregard the corporation's separate legal existence and seek to recover from the stockholders under the doctrine of "piercing the corporate veil."

Responsibilities of Officers and Directors

Officers and directors owe a fiduciary duty of care to the corporation and its stockholders. In this, they must exercise reasonable business judgment to advance the interests of the corporation.

They also owe a fiduciary duty of loyalty to the corporation and its stockholders. Thus, they must always act in the best interest of the corporation; they may not, for example, take personal advantage of a business opportunity that comes to their attention in their capacity as a director or officer.

Moreover, they must disclose any personal interest they may have when considering matters at directors' meetings or in functioning as officers. Further, directors may not vote on issues in which they have a personal interest and, similarly, officers may not act in such circumstances.

Directors and officers who act in accordance with these responsibilities will generally not be liable to the corporation or its stockholders. Moreover, except in cases of insolvency or where the corporation is approaching of insolvency, directors generally do not owe a fiduciary duty to persons other than the corporation and its stockholders in making business decisions. On the other hand, the corporation will almost always be responsible for the acts of its directors, officers or employees acting within the scope of their authority.

Generally, neither directors nor officers will have personal criminal or civil liability for the criminal or civil acts of the corporation in which they do not participate or which they do not explicitly or implicitly authorize, as the corporation is considered itself to be criminally liable. A director or officer is always responsible for his or her own criminal or wrongful civil acts.

The directors and officers are also generally not liable to the creditors of the corporation absent personal wrong doing, such as self-dealing or embezzlement.

While the directors and officers may not defraud creditors or conceal the corporation's weak financial condition from them, they will not incur liability solely on account of the corporation's inability to satisfy its debts. Recently, however, some courts have expanded the fiduciary duties of directors and officers when a corporation becomes insolvent or approaches insolvency to include not only the corporation and its stockholders, but the corporation's creditors as well.

Just as with stockholders, the directors and officers are best protected from liability for corporate debts and acts by respecting all corporate formalities, maintaining complete and accurate financial books and records, obtaining full and frank financial information before approving transactions (particularly if the corporation is approaching insolvency) and maintaining internal accounting controls that enable them to manage the acts and assets of the corporation.

Chapter 45: Financial and Tax Matters

Corporate law in the United States with respect to non-publicly traded companies has few mandatory rules regarding the financial management of the corporation.

Approval of Balance Sheet

It is not required (or customary) that the stockholders approve the balance sheet and annual profit and loss statement. Moreover, the annual balance sheet is not published except in the case of corporations whose shares are publicly traded.

In addition, it is not customary or necessary for the stockholders to release the board of directors from liability for their actions.

Reserves

US law establishes no compulsory reserves of any kind. Generally accepted accounting principles, however, require the setting-up of certain reserves, such as for bad debts or current litigation, on a corporation's balance sheet.

Dividends

In most states, dividends may be paid out of accumulated profits (or "earned surplus") and out of paid-in surplus. In Delaware, it is also permitted to pay dividends out of current profits even if losses in earlier years have impaired the corporation's capital.

A "dividend" out of paid-in surplus where there is a current and cumulative loss would not be considered to be a "dividend" for tax purposes, however, since the company would have no earnings and profits; rather, it would be treated as a return of capital.

Tax Matters

There are two kinds of corporations for federal income tax purposes. One kind is governed by Subchapter C of the Internal Revenue Code, or "C Corporation," and the other is a "small business corporation," or "S corporation," for which a Subchapter S election under the Internal Revenue Code is in effect. A C corporation must itself pay income tax. Thus, the profits of a C corporation are subject to double taxation, first, on the corporate level and, second, on the level of the recipient stockholder.

An S corporation is not subject to income tax at the corporate level. Rather, its profits are directly allocated to its stockholders, who must then report the income and expenses on their own tax returns. To qualify as an S corporation, a corporation must have been founded under US law and have no more than 75 stockholders, who must either be a natural person other than a non-resident alien, the estate of a natural person, or a qualified trust. Furthermore, an S corporation may not have more than one class of stock. An S corporation is generally not suitable for non-US investors.

Chapter 46: Limited Liability Companies

In addition to corporations, the laws of all states in the United States provide for the organization of limited liability companies, or LLCs. LLCs do not have any limitation on the minimum (i.e., one member is acceptable) or maximum number of members or the transferability of shares.

They are a hybrid entity, essentially comprised of the more favourable attributes of partnerships and corporations. Like US corporations, LLCs are extremely flexible. Usually, the choice between an LLC and a corporation will often be driven by tax considerations, as discussed below.

Types of LLCs

The flexibility available with a limited liability company is useful in meeting the particular needs and objectives of either a non-US investor or a US entrepreneur.

An LLC can be, and often is, customized for each client. However, there is a cost associated with customization, and ultimately an LLC may prove significantly more expensive to organize than a corporation.

There are four "model" LLC formats: a "corporate model," a "partnership model" and two hybrid models; one with "managers" and one with "officers." These models are more fully set forth below. Note that the choice among these models relates to their structure and management, not to their tax treatment, which is entirely independent of their structure.

1. Corporate Model LLC

A corporate model LLC is organized and managed similarly to a US corporation. The owners of an LLC are its members, and are analogous to a corporation's stockholders. The members are issued membership units, which are analogous to shares.

A corporate model LLC will have a board of directors elected by the members. As in a corporation, the board manages the LLC and establishes business policies by acting collectively that is, making decisions as a group. The board elects officers, who conduct the day-to-day affairs of the LLC, represent it in dealing with third parties and otherwise act as authorized by the board of directors.

The officers thus serve the same functions as officers in a US corporation. Profits are allocated in accordance with unit ownership (although this may be varied) and there will normally be no complicated provisions, or special allocations, allocating profits and losses. Thus the corporate model LLC agreement is a rather compact document.

The members will typically only vote for the election of directors or on fundamental matters such as a merger or dissolution of the LLC. The principal choices relate to the number and identity of the directors and officers, amount and nature of capital contributions, and any fundamental items to be resolved by the members.

2. Partnership Model

In contrast, the partnership model does not attempt to replicate the features of a corporation. It may be used when the owners of the LLC are individuals or entities; it is a particularly appropriate model when all of the members are active in the business of the LLC.

The partnership model is managed directly by its members, as in the case of a US general partnership (but without the liability of general partners).

Each member may represent the LLC in its dealings with third parties. Although it is possible to limit representation and management to fewer than all members, in many states such a limitation may not be binding on third parties who are unaware of it. Thus, it is typically more efficient to use the "hybrid model with managers," as discussed below, to achieve management by less than all members.

Unlike the corporate model, profits and losses may be allocated other than by way of percentage ownership. Thus, a key question in the partnership model is how profits and losses are to be allocated. If special allocations are employed, fairly lengthy tax provisions are often inserted to ensure that the allocations are respected by the IRS. This may add considerably to the length and complexity of the LLC agreement.

3. Hybrid Models

Since both "hybrid" LLCs are managed by the members and so, similar to the partnership model, neither has a board of directors. In both models, the members establish company policy acting as a group but the members do not directly represent and operate the LLC in its day-to-day business. Rather, they elect other persons to conduct the day-to-day business of the LLC and represent it in dealings with third parties.

In one hybrid model, this person is designated as the manager (who may or may not be a member). In the other hybrid model, these persons are designated as officers, thus mirroring the corporate model, but without an intervening board of directors. A manager will generally exercise greater authority than an officer, as described below.

We generally recommend the use of a manager or officers. Having the LLC represented by the members with respect to third parties often proves cumbersome in practice. Third parties are generally more comfortable dealing with officers or managers, and the members may not wish to have daily management responsibility.
Special profit and loss allocations can be utilized, as with the partnership model.

4.   Single Member Limited Liability Companies

Single member LLCs may take any of the foregoing forms. The preferred governance model for a single member LLC may depend in part upon whether the single member is an individual or a corporation or other business entity, and also in part upon whether the owner of the LLC is US or a non-US citizen or entity.

If the sole owner of the LLC is an individual, there is no need to have a board of directors, and the LLC could be managed by the sole member. However, we generally still recommend the use of a manager or officers (even if the sole member is the manager or president) because, unless a manager or officers are present, the LLC must be represented by the

186

member in that capacity with respect to third parties. Without the use of the title of manager or president, it may be difficult for the member to avoid treating the LLC as his or her alter ego and so there is some chance that the LLC could fall a foul of the doctrine of piercing the corporate veil doctrine.

If the owner is a corporation, the owner may prefer the familiar structure of the corporate model LLC. Furthermore, a non-US investor may prefer to have the LLC managed by one or more managers who would act similarly to managing directors of certain non-US companies. In this case, the manager or managers would not act primarily through meetings but would individually represent the LLC in its dealings with third parties.

Chapter 47: Formation of Limited Liability Companies

Place of Formation

There is no national LLC law and so regulation of the formation and operation of LLCs is, as in the context of corporations, left largely to the individual states.

Unlike, for example, the European practice of requiring a company to be organized under the law of the jurisdiction in which its principal place of business is located, a US LLC, like a US corporation, may be organized under the laws of one state and yet have its principal place of business elsewhere so long as it "qualifies to do business" in each state in which it operates.

This allows investors to choose the optimal state law. Sometimes there is no great significance to the jurisdiction chosen, but Delaware law is considerably better suited for companies with multiple investors. On the other hand (and as discussed earlier with respect to formation of corporations), a Delaware company doing business in just one state (other than

Delaware) will have to pay two annual franchise fees. This factor may be sufficient reason to organize under the law of the state in which the company will be doing business.

The laws of Illinois and many other states are nearly as convenient and flexible as Delaware law notwithstanding certain disadvantages, particularly as regards the corporate model, especially if the LLC is to have more than one member. Again, because of Delaware's preeminence, any references to legal rules throughout this chapter are to those of Delaware, unless otherwise noted.

Certificate of Formation

A limited liability company is organized by registering its certificate of formation or, in certain states, articles of organization, with the Secretary of State of the state in which it is to be organized. The certificate of formation may be executed by any one person (frequently an attorney) acting on behalf of the future members and so it need not be executed by a non-US investor.

Name

The name of the limited liability company must end with the word "Limited Liability Company" or, in many states, the abbreviation "LLC." The name also must be distinguishable from other existing or reserved entity names.

Purpose

This may be stated in very broad terms under the Delaware statute, usually including "any activity permitted by law" without any indication of the business in which the company will actually engage. In certain other states, the purpose may be stated broadly, but there must be some indication of the specific type of business in which the company will actually engage. This purpose may be expanded in the future by means of an amendment of the certificate of formation.

Procedures

The principal steps in organizing a Delaware limited liability company are the following:

The certificate of formation is executed (by one or more "authorized persons") and filed with the Secretary of State of the state of organization.

The members normally enter into a "limited liability company agreement" (or, in other states, an "operating agreement") to govern the operation of the LLC. The LLC agreement is a private document among the members. A typical LLC agreement covers such matters as the formation of the company, its business, the members and their capital contributions, the management of the company, the means by which the members may act the allocation of profits, and the dissolution of the company and termination of the operating agreement.

If the LLC has a single member, the LLC agreement is quite simple. If the LLC has two or more members, it is more like a joint venture and the LLC agreement often includes other provisions typical of a joint venture agreement or stockholders agreement, such as limitations on the ability of the members to transfer their interests and provision for resolution of deadlocks. The investor-members "subscribe" for membership interests in the LLC. Membership interests may also be called membership units, and may be represented by certificates or not at the election of the members.

The managers or directors, if any, are appointed by the members.

The members, and managers or directors, if any, hold an initial meeting, which may also be accomplished by means of a "consent resolution," (that is, a written resolution signed by all members, managers or directors, as applicable, without a meeting) at which the following action is typically taken:

(i) Approve the actions of the person who signed the certificate of formation.

(ii) Appoint the officers, if any, of the LLC.

(iii) Appoint a registered or resident agent (as with corporations, this may be a corporate service provider).

(iv) Authorize the officers or, in the absence of officers, other appropriate persons, to qualify the LLC to do business in whatever other state may be necessary because of the nature of the limited liability company's activities in that state.

(v) Adopt an accounting method and fiscal year if not covered in the operating agreement.

(vi) Approve opening a bank account.

(vii) Appoint independent auditors, if any. Auditors are not required under any US law for a limited liability company although a limited liability company's banks and other principal creditors will usually require financial statements prepared, reviewed by, certified or audited by independent auditors.

(viii) Approve the operating agreement. This approval is not mandatory.

Chapter 48: Membership Interests and Capital

The ownership interests of the members in a LLC, formally known as membership interests or membership units, may be represented by membership certificates or may merely be reflected in the operating agreement or a membership register maintained by the company. Membership certificates may not be in bearer form.

Membership interests may be issued for cash, personal or real property, an agreement to contribute cash or property in the future, and past or, in most states, future services. No appraisal or court approval is required for valuing members' contributions of any kind or for issuing membership interests. The good faith determination of the value of a contribution by the members is sufficient.

A member's interest in the company does not have to be in any way proportional to the value of its contribution.

Voting and Other Rights

A member does not have to be given a right to vote or otherwise participate in the management of the company, although the right of a member to obtain certain information about the financial and other affairs of the company cannot be restricted in most states. Members and membership units may be given differing and non-proportional rights to participate in the profits and losses, distributions and equity of the company

The flexibility offered by a limited liability company in this regard is limited only by the imagination of the parties and their counsel, although US tax laws impose certain requirements in order that an allocation of profits and losses is recognized for US tax purposes.

Role of Capital

As stated above in the context of corporations, in general, the concept of capital is both more flexible and less important with respect to US business entities than those of other jurisdictions. The emphasis in the United States tends to be on promoting the growth of the company rather than preserving its capital. For LLCs, capital is an accounting, and not legal, concept. As such it plays an insignificant procedural role in the formation and operation of LLCs.

Chapter 49: Limited Liability Company Structure

A limited liability company must have at least one member but, as noted in earlier chapter of this book, its management structure generally may be determined in whatever manner the members desire. The member or members may operate the company directly (as in the partnership model) or may themselves appoint officers or managers to operate the daily affairs of the LLC. If there are multiple members with differing equity interests, member management with officers to conduct the day-to-day business may be quite convenient since the members will automatically vote in accordance with their respective voting percentage interests.

Reflecting such interests through board membership in a corporate model can be somewhat clumsy. If the members do not wish to manage the company directly, they may provide for the election of a manager or managers to conduct the ordinary business affairs of the company.

This approach may be familiar to non-US investors. In some cases, the members may choose to have a corporation-type management structure, with both a board of directors and officers. This structure has the advantage of appearing familiar to those persons in the United States with whom the company will deal who may be more familiar with corporations than limited liability companies. Each of these management structures is described below.

Members

The members hold the ultimate authority in the company. Thus, under any management structure, they will have to approve any extraordinary action, such as a merger of the limited liability company into another entity, the sale of all or substantially all of the assets of the company, or its dissolution. However, the percentage of members who must approve such extraordinary acts is determined by the operating agreement. In the absence of an appropriate provision, approval would normally be by majority vote in most states.

The members may act in a variety of ways

Under the corporate and hybrid models, the operating agreement provides that members act through an actual meeting at which the members may be present in person, by proxy, or by conference telephone (that is, any telephone arrangement through which members may be heard by all other members).

Members may also act in lieu of a meeting through consent in writing executed by a majority of the members unless state law or the operating agreement requires a larger number.

This is a considerable convenience, especially where the company is wholly-owned by a US or non-US investor, since it avoids the charade of holding a "meeting" of the sole member. In a partnership model, the members actively participate in the business and each has the authority to make decisions for the LLC individually, without a meeting. In this case, there may still be provision for meetings of the members for consideration of extraordinary matters where decisions are to be taken by the members as a whole.

Dissociation of a Member

The term "dissociation" is used in conjunction with LLCs and partnerships in the United States. It generally refers to any circumstance under which a member or partner ceases to have that status, which may arise in a variety of situations.

Transfer

If a member transfers his or her entire interest, he or she will no longer be a member. Although this is treated as dissociation in a number of LLC statutes, this is not typically the case because there will be a substitute member and so none of the issues discussed below are likely to arise.

Voluntary Resignation

Because LLC statutes are often derived from partnership predecessors, they used to permit a member to resign at will, although an LLC statute might also provide that this voluntary resignation might be wrongful or in violation of the operating agreement. This situation prevails in a number of states.

In Delaware, however, a member only has the right to resign if it is stated in the operating agreement. Absent special circumstances, we generally recommend against permitting members to resign voluntarily in order to insure the stability of the business.

Death or Dissolution

A member will cease to be such upon the member's death (in the case of an individual) or dissolution (in the case of an entity). In a corporation, neither event would have any automatic impact (the heirs or successors would simply succeed as owners of the shares) absent a contrary provision in a stockholders agreement.

Under many LLC statutes, death or dissolution still results in dissolution of the LLC although the LLC may be continued, and liquidation of the business avoided, if the remaining members decide to do so. In Delaware and some other states, death or dissolution does not automatically result in dissolution of the LLC. However, even in the case of a corporation, it may not be practical to continue to operate with the heirs or successors as owner.

This is particularly true of a business in which the participation of each member is important, in which case it would not be appropriate to have a passive investor as a member. In this case, the only practical alternative to dissolution or liquidation of the LLC may be to have the LLC redeem the interest of the dissociated member.

Chapter 50: Bankruptcy or Insolvency

It is customary to provide for the automatic dissociation of a member that becomes bankrupt or otherwise is insolvent. However, such a provision may not be binding on a bankruptcy court. A trustee in bankruptcy may have the right to avoid such a provision if the trustee is not satisfied that the provision for the redemption of the membership interest is fair to creditors of the bankrupt member.

Redemption and Valuation

A threshold question with respect to redemption is whether the LLC is likely to have the liquidity to pay for the dissociated member's interest regardless of its valuation. Under most LLC statutes, one may provide for a payout of the redemption amount over an extended period of time, but even the incurrence of that type of liability may put a significant strain on the business.

Liquidity may be enhanced by appropriate planning, such as obtaining life insurance for the benefit of the LLC on the life of each individual member.

Assuming liquidity is adequate, there remains the problem of valuing the dissociated member's interest. One may always look to the book value of the interest (or the member's capital account in the context of an LLC) but, in a going concern, this is unlikely to reflect the full fair value of the interest.

There are a number of other ways in which a membership interest may be valued, such as:

1. An annual valuation of the business or at least of its key assets. The principal risk in this approach is that the members may fail to do this on an annual basis, in which case the valuation may be significantly out of date.
2. Valuation by formula. A business is often valued in relation to an indicative financial or operating performance measure or anticipated income stream. If the members are confident that past history is predictive of the future, one may value the company, and therefore the interest, as a multiple of the LLC's recent earnings (a three-year period is a frequent reference). A host of relevant financial or operating measures (e.g., earnings multiple, sales multiple, number of customers, number of stores) may be appropriate for valuation purposes.
3. Third-party valuation. It is possible to have the business valued by an individual knowledgeable about such businesses (who should be identified at least by title in the operating agreement) or by a professional organization, such as an accounting firm, a business valuation professional, or an investment banker.

Chapter 51: Directors, Officers and Managers

A limited liability company may, but is not required to, act through directors, officers and/or managers. Directors, officers and managers are normally individuals but there is no general requirement that they be citizens or residents of the United States or a particular state (although visa requirements do apply to non-citizens and non-residents). None need be members.

Board of Directors

A corporate model LLC has a board of directors elected by the members which often operates in a manner similar to that of a board of directors of a corporation.

Thus, the directors usually make decisions and set policy acting as a group, meeting in person or through the use of a conference telephone. They may also act through consent resolutions with whatever majority is specified in the operating agreement.

In addition, unlike a corporation, there is no requirement that directors participate personally in meetings. Therefore, an operating agreement may provide that directors can act through proxies or may provide for alternate directors or substitute directors, however unusual in the United States.

Officers

Limited liability companies organized on a corporate or hybrid model may provide for officers to actually conduct the company's business. As noted above, this may be advantageous in dealing with parties who are used to dealing with the "president" of an entity.

The officers will be appointed by the members or board of directors (depending on the model chosen) and will typically be removable by them at any time. Officers generally consist of a president and secretary, and possibly one or more vice-presidents, and a treasurer.

The president typically acts as chief executive officer of the LLC although one may opt for a chairman of the board of directors to hold this position. As chief executive, the president has broad powers to represent the LLC in the ordinary course of its business. However, any significant corporate action, including most dealings with real estate and with financial institutions, requires express approval by the board of directors, unless otherwise provided in the operating agreement.

Managers

In a hybrid model LLC in which the members elect a manager or managers to operate the business; the managers generally exercise broader authority than would persons designated as officers. In most states, managers may exercise all company powers not reserved to the members in the operating agreement.

Moreover, in many states, third parties are entitled to rely on the broad authority of a manager unless the third party has actual knowledge of limitations imposed on the manager's authority in the operating agreement. Thus, it is more difficult to restrict the actual or apparent authority of one designated as a "manager" than would be the case of one designated as "president." Managers may themselves represent the company or may delegate authority for the day-to-day conduct of the company's business to other employees.

Chapter 52: Governance of the Limited Liability Company

Liability of Members

Businesses are conducted as limited liability companies primarily in order to secure the benefits of limited liability. Accordingly, the investment that a member makes in a company is necessarily at risk but the member ought not to be responsible for the liabilities or losses of the company beyond that investment. However, even in the case of a corporation, creditors may "pierce the corporate veil" and hold the stockholders liable for corporate debts under some circumstances.

The limited liability company is a relatively new form of entity in the United States, but it seems likely that the same principles will be applied to them as apply to corporations.

Thus, if the separate existence of the limited liability company is not respected, there is a risk that creditors are able to disregard the company and recover from the members any damages.

Responsibilities of Officers and Directors

The subject of fiduciary duties owed by managers in a manager-managed LLC, or members in a member-managed LLC, is an emerging and complex topic, the details of which are beyond the scope of this book. However, the Delaware limited liability company statute was recently amended to clarify that the parties may define by contract their responsibilities and duties, including fiduciary duties.

In particular, the Delaware LLC statute provides that a "member's or manager's or other person's duties may be expanded or restricted or eliminated by provisions in the limited liability company agreement; provided that the limited liability company agreement may not eliminate the implied contractual covenant of good faith and fair dealing."

Furthermore, the statute provides that, unless otherwise specified in the LLC agreement, a person (e.g., a member or manager) is not liable to the LLC or another person (e.g., another member or manager) for breach of fiduciary duty for the person's good faith reliance on the provisions of the LLC agreement. This suggests that disgruntled members would need to bring claims for breach of contract, rather than breach of fiduciary (or other) duties owed if those duties are not specified in the LLC agreement.

Chapter 53: Financial Matters

In the United States, the law governing limited liability companies has few mandatory rules with respect to the financial management of the LLC.

Approval of Balance Sheet and Management

It is not required (or customary) that the members approve the balance sheet and annual profit and loss statement. Moreover, the annual balance sheet is not published except in the case of companies whose shares are publicly traded (which are almost always corporations, not limited liability companies). In addition, it is not customary or necessary for the members annually to approve the actions of the managers or officers or to release the managers or officers from liability for their actions.

Reserves

US law establishes no compulsory reserves of any kind. Generally accepted accounting principles may require the setting-up of certain reserves, such as for bad debts, on a company's balance sheet, however.

Distributions

Limited liability company law in the United States has few mandatory rules with respect to the financial management of the company but distributions may only be made if they would not impair the Company's financial condition.

Profit and Loss Allocations

In a limited liability company, profits and losses can be allocated among the members without regard to the members' equity interests or voting power (a so-called "special allocation").

However, if an allocation of profits and/or losses not in accordance with equity interests is to be respected for US income tax purposes, the tax allocation must reflect the actual economic relationship between the members.

This rule only rarely presents problems in practice but may require the inclusion of lengthy tax provisions in the operating agreement.

Tax Matters

There is no special tax regime for limited liability companies as such. A limited liability company in the United States may be taxed as a corporation or a partnership (or a disregarded entity, in the case of a single member LLC) at its option. If taxed as a corporation, the company must itself pay taxes (at corporate rates) on its income.

If taxed as a partnership, the company is not itself subject to US income taxation but only acts as a conduit. This tax treatment is determined simply by checking the appropriate box on the LLC's tax return. It is not affected in any way by the model chosen. In other words, a corporate model may be taxed as a partnership and a partnership model may be taxed as a corporation.

From the point of view of a non-US investor, structuring a limited liability company as a partnership will cause the investor/member to be taxed as if it were operating in the United States through a branch, but at the same time enjoy limited liability. Such an arrangement will likely subject the investor to the US branch profits tax, which can subject a non-US investor to higher current US taxes and a loss of flexibility in timing the payment of dividends. A detailed discussion of whether operating as a branch is advantageous is beyond the scope of this book and should be addressed in the context of each particular investor, its country of origin, and the nature of its proposed investment or operations in the United States.

Chapter 54: Limited Partnerships and Limited Liability

Partnerships

Generally, a partnership is an association of two or more persons to carry on a business for profit. A partnership is typically a pass-through vehicle, that is, it is not itself subject to taxation.

Rather, its income is taxed directly to the partners. However, if desired, a partnership may elect to be subject to tax as if it were a corporation.

Partnerships may be either a general partnership or a limited partnership. All of the partners in a general partnership, the general partners, are entirely liable for the debts of the partnership. Because of the focus upon limited liability in US business entities, the general partnership will not be discussed herein.

Limited partnerships consist of two species of partners: general partners, who are subject to unlimited liability, and limited partners, whose liability is limited to their contribution to the limited partnership. General partners have the same rights, liabilities, and powers as partners in general partnerships. Thus, the ordinary principles of partnership apply; general partners manage the partnership, share in the partnership's profits and losses and have unlimited personal liability. In contrast, the limited partners' liability is limited to their investment in the business. The desirable limited liability status of limited partners, however, comes at a price; limited partners generally have to abstain from participating in managing the business. Therefore, limited partnerships provide individuals the opportunity to invest in a business in return for the share of the profits and still avoid personal liability for the business's debts.

It is common to structure limited partnerships with a corporate general partner. Although limited partners normally may not directly manage the limited partnership without jeopardizing their limited liability, they may engage in management indirectly through a corporate general partner. Delaware and a number of other states specifically provide that a limited partner's acting as a director or officer of a corporate general partner will not constitute participation in management for liability purposes.

The investor or investors may be the shareholder or shareholders of the corporate general partner and also be the limited partner or limited partners in the limited partnership. In this structure, the investors would control the corporate general partner by appointing its directors and officers. While the corporate general partner's assets would be at risk, this structure means that the investors would have limited their liability to their respective investments in the enterprise.

Unlike an ordinary general partnership, a limited partnership may not be formed by anything less than deliberate action. In every state, there are statutory requirements which have to be complied with to form a limited partnership.

Instead of individually drafting their respective limited partnership acts in isolation, almost all states have enacted the Revised Uniform Limited Partnership Act.

Thus, the differences from state to state are minute. Most state statutes require a limited partnership to file a certificate with the information specified by its state of organization, to appoint and maintain an agent for service of process in the state, and to make filings if it amends or cancels its certificate.

Out-of-state limited partnerships generally will be permitted to be licensed to do business upon filing the appropriate application with the state where it wishes to expand its business.

Recently, almost all states have enacted legislation allowing general partnerships to register and thereby shield their partners from some or all liabilities. In Delaware, Illinois and certain other states, the partners will not have any personal liability for any partnership obligation incurred after the partnership is registered as a "limited liability partnership." (The liability shield is more limited in other states, and limited liability partnerships are not available for commercial investments in, for example, New York.) If an investment is contemplated in a state providing a full liability shield for registered limited liability partnerships, this alternative should be considered as an investment vehicle, particularly where investment through a partnership is otherwise advantageous.

General and limited partnerships have long been used for joint ventures but, with the advent of limited liability companies, their use has declined considerably.

Nonetheless, limited partnerships are still used for ventures operating in certain states where that form may significantly reduce state taxes on the parties and by non-US investors for whom there may be a non-US tax benefit to operating in the United States in partnership form.

215

Chapter 55: Choice of Entity

Parties seeking to access the US market will often debate whether to utilize a corporation or an LLC. While an LLC is similar to a corporation from a limited liability perspective, and both entities are well respected business organizations, an LLC may be preferable to the corporate form because of its flexibility and its tax attributes. It is generally easier to provide for different financial and membership interests in an LLC than in a corporation as, for example, ownership interests in an LLC may be expressed as units (essentially equivalent to shares) or as a percentage interest in the entity.

Currently, however, an LLC's membership interests cannot be traded publicly. Thus, with the exception of a publicly traded entity, an LLC may almost always be substituted for a corporation.

An LLC also enjoys advantages over a corporation with respect to its tax attributes. While the operation of a venture through a corporation typically will involve two levels of taxation (to the corporation itself and then to its stockholders), an LLC may elect to be taxed as if it were a corporation or as if it were a pass-through entity like a partnership. The tax considerations are likely to drive the determination of whether an LLC rather than a corporation is the preferred vehicle for the US subsidiary.

However, since both an LLC and a corporation generally provide for limited liability of its owners, an LLC may be preferable to a corporation for the US subsidiary from a flexibility perspective. Moreover, as mentioned above, an LLC can assume the structure of a corporation, and thus can have officers and directors. However, for certain non-US investors, utilization of a partnership may provide significant tax advantages.

In addition to those potential tax benefits, a limited partnership or a limited liability partnership provides the benefits of limited liability of a corporation or LLC. Moreover, a limited partnership is an equally-respected business entity in the US business community and market.

This structure is commercially feasible, increasingly used by purely US-owned business and provides limited liability. The limited partnership form generally poses no significant problem with respect to supplier, customer or bank acceptance.

Further, by operating through a Delaware limited partnership with a corporate general partner, the investor or investors would be shielded from direct liability (which would be limited to their capital contributions to the entity).

Use of a corporation as a general partner in a limited partnership should likewise result in limited liability for the corporation's stockholders even though the corporation itself has unlimited liability for the obligations of the limited partnership.

Chapter 56: Branches, Subsidiaries and Joint Venture

It is possible for a non-US corporation to operate a branch office in the United States, but there are significant disadvantages to a branch, particularly with respect to its tax treatment and liability.

Branches of non-US corporations are not subject to federal regulation or registration requirements. However, each state will require a "foreign" corporation to qualify before "doing business" in that state. A corporation will be considered "foreign" if it is organized under the laws of another country or another US state, and so this is not a requirement imposed solely upon non-US investors. "Doing business" is a technical term that implies a substantial presence in the state. Thus, examples of "doing business" include the ownership or leasing of real property, the maintenance of a stock of goods for local sale, employees, etc. Selling products to local customers, either directly or through an independent sales representative or distributor, would not in itself constitute "doing business."

States actually exercise little control over the qualification process other than to ensure that the qualifying entity's name is not confusingly similar to an already registered entity and that all registration fees and taxes are paid (qualification is basically a form of taxation). In most states, qualification for a non-US corporation consists of a relatively easy application, a registration fee, and a notarized or legalized copy of the corporation's articles of incorporation (in English or accompanied by a certified translation). The burdens deriving from being considered as "doing business" in a state are not particularly onerous, although it likely also results in an obligation to file state income tax returns and pay related taxes.

Subsidiaries

Most often, investment in the United States is done via a subsidiary (whether as the vehicle to implement an acquisition or to conduct day-to-day operations in connection with a direct investment by means other than an acquisition).

Recall that the formation of business entities is not subject to extensive federal regulation or registration procedures. Corporations, LLCs and other entities are organized under state law. As discussed previously, it is fairly easy to organize a corporation, partnership or an LLC. No administrative or court approval or appraisal of non-cash contributions is required, and so either form of entity may be organized in 48 hours or less.

A US subsidiary will provide significant flexibility for US operations and protection for the investor. A subsidiary provides great financial flexibility and the existence of a US subsidiary will generally not subject the foreign parent to jurisdiction in US courts. However, exposure may arise if the plaintiff successfully pierces the corporate veil.

US Joint Ventures and Strategic Alliances

The term joint venture or strategic alliance encompasses any ongoing cooperative relationship between businesses. As such, a joint venture may assume any one of many forms from that of a purely contractual relationship to that of organizing a new entity, and may be referred to as a joint venture or strategic alliance.

While a range of forms constitute a joint venture, joint ventures typically involve some sharing of profits and an ongoing relationship. Where the parties to the arrangement determine that it will be in their best interest to form a separate legal entity for purposes of conducting the venture, it will be important to consider the features and attributes (in particular, tax attributes) of the available types of entities described earlier in this section in more detail.

Limited liability companies are frequently utilized given their flexibility with respect to addressing financial, tax and management issues.

Chapter 57: Intellectual Property and Terrorism Threat

See below for information on key security and political risks which UK businesses may face when operating in the United States.

As at the time of publishing this book, we are not aware of any issues causing critical concern to UK customers in the areas of organised crime, corruption, physical security or political risk. We do, however, wish to highlight two topics that we consider most relevant:

- Terrorism and
- Intellectual property.

Terrorism Threat

The US Department of Homeland Security (DHS) operates a threat advisory system offering information on the current terrorist threat level in the US, and advice on protective measures.

The Centre for the Protection of National Infrastructure also provides protective security advice to businesses.

Intellectual Property

IP rights are territorial, that is they only give protection in the countries where they are granted or registered. If you are thinking about trading internationally, then you should consider registering your IP rights in your export markets.

US intellectual property law is well-developed and offers robust protection for businesses operating in the United States. USA and UK intellectual property regimes are broadly similar but not identical. For example US patents are awarded on a 'first-to-invent' basis, rather than not the 'first-to-file' basis in the UK. The number of costly intellectual property infringement litigation cases in the US has increased markedly in recent years. The main government office responsible for intellectual property is the US Patent and Trademark Office (USPTO), which issues patents and trademarks and governs their use.

Copyrights must be registered with the Copyright Office of the Library of Congress. Protection of trade secrets can vary from state to state, though most adhere to the Uniform Trade Secrets Act (UTSA). Businesses which have suffered intellectual property infringement have recourse to the domestic legal system.

Chapter 58: Bribery and Corruption

Bribery is illegal and has no place in British business, at home or abroad. It is an offence for UK nationals and bodies incorporated under UK law to bribe anywhere in the world. From 01 July 2011 the Bribery Act makes it an offence for commercial organisations carrying on a business in the UK to fail to prevent bribery on their behalf by employees and other associated persons.

UK enforcement is increasing, with a number of UK nationals and companies recently fined or imprisoned for their involvement in overseas corruption.

Overseas corruption also hurts honest companies and raises the costs of doing business. Surveys regularly show that a significant number of UK companies have lost business to a bribing competitor or turned down overseas opportunities due to overseas corruption.

The UK is working with our peers at the OECD, UN and other international bodies to level the global playing field and confront local cultures of corruption.

The UN has recently launched a new initiative called Tools and Resources for Anti-Corruption Knowledge (TRACK). This includes a legal library containing laws, jurisprudence and other information on anti-corruption authorities from over 175 States worldwide, indexed and searchable according to each provision of the UN Convention Against Convention (e.g. official embezzlement, prohibitions against bribery, procurement, etc).

Bribery Act 2010

The Bribery Act 2010 came into force on 01 July 2011 and, following extensive consultation with business, UK Government has published the Bribery Act guidance. The intention of the guidance is to provide commercial organisations with the information they need to put in place to prevent bribery on their behalf. Alongside the full guidance, there is also a quick start guide which it is hoped will be particularly useful to SMEs.

The Director of the Serious Fraud Office and the Director of Public Prosecutions have published guidance on their approach to prosecutorial decision-making in respect of offences under the Act. During the consultation period, there was particular interest in a number of areas:

Hospitality and Promotional Expenditure

The Bribery Act does not prohibit hospitality, and the Ministry of Justice guidance confirms that hospitality is allowed as long as it is reasonable and proportionate. The independent prosecution authority guidance confirms that excessively lavish hospitality is an important consideration in the decision on whether to prosecute. Other public interest factors include whether the hospitality was not clearly connected with a legitimate business activity, or was concealed.

Facilitation payments

UK law has never provided an exemption for facilitation payments (small bribes to secure routine government action). The Bribery Act does not change that position. We believe they also undermine corporate anti-bribery procedures and confuse the anti-bribery message to employees and business partners.

The Ministry of Justice guidance makes clear that payments specifically permitted or required under local law are not bribes (e.g. as part of a transparent fast-track scheme for business visas). The Ministry of Justice guidance also makes clear that, where payments are made in response to immediate threats to life or limb, the general common law defence of duress may be available.

Furthermore, the independent prosecution authority guidance makes clear that they will have regard to the public interest in prosecution of facilitation payments particularly where they are paid, for example, where the payer was in a vulnerable position because of the circumstances where the payment was demanded (e.g. demands by armed militia at roadblocks).

Chapter 59: Human Rights and Physical Security

UK Government believes that free trade and economic growth promote development and respect for human rights. We encourage British businesses to be aware of their potential impacts on human rights.

As British business expands overseas we will need to ensure that this success is not achieved at the expense of human rights.

We encourage you to strive to promote competitive and transparent conditions for doing business by spreading internationally agreed standards of responsible business and best practice.

Good business and respect for human rights should be mutually reinforcing. Respect for human rights helps legitimate, sustainable business; it creates stable operating environments and sustainable markets with lessened risk of reputational damage or of litigation. And good business practice has a positive impact on human rights; it sets standards of behaviour, improves governance, provides livelihoods free of abuse, removes incentives to abuse, helps tackle disadvantage, maximises skills and sustainable employability and strengthens communities.

Protect your people, your information and your skills

Protective security advice is aimed at reducing the vulnerability of your business and staff to national security threats, including those such as terrorism, cyber attack or espionage.

The most effective way to secure your business against these is to use a combination of measures covering physical, personnel and information security; including cyber security.

A good source of guidance is the UK's Centre for the Protection of National Infrastructure, (CPNI). This body advises businesses and organisations within the UK's national infrastructure about protective security. Amongst their advice you can find a range of generic security measures that can help protect your business interests overseas from potential threats such as terrorism and espionage. A summary of these is set out below.

Information security (including cyber security)

Almost every business relies on the confidentiality, integrity and availability of its data. Protecting information, whether it is held electronically or by other means, should be at the heart of the organisation's security planning

Cyber crime in the "virtual" environment is today the world's fastest-growing crime sector. Your cyber security is paramount if you are beginning to trade overseas or expanding your overseas business.

CPNI provides a range of guidance documents and technical notes aimed at improving practices and raising awareness of current issues related to information security.

Such measures can defend against electronic attack, instil good practice processes, improve process control, and system security alike.

Physical security is important in protecting against a range of threats and addressing vulnerability. You should put in place security measures to remove or reduce your vulnerabilities to as low as reasonably practicable, bearing in mind the need to consider safety as a priority at all times.

Advice on Physical security measures is provided by UK Government on ways to protect buildings, contents, equipment and so on. These include basic good housekeeping, CCTV/intruder alarms/access control systems, parking and traffic controls, mail screening and lighting.

Personnel security

Personnel security is a system of policies and procedures which seek to manage the risk of staff or contractors exploiting their legitimate access to an organisation's assets or premises for unauthorised purposes. These purposes can encompass many forms of criminal activity, from minor theft through to terrorism.

The CPNI website includes guidance on how such risks, including those from "insiders", can be minimised. It also covers pre-employment screening, personal document verification, security culture, and ongoing personnel security measures and personnel risk assessments.

Chapter 60: Conclusion

Business people are generally expected to dress smartly. Western business courtesies should be observed, although Americans tend to be less formal than Europeans. Appointments and punctuality are expected procedure and business cards are widely used. Dates in America are written month-day-year.

It is quite common for meetings to be held over lunch, although the prohibitive cost of eating out in Washington, DC at traditional business venues means that some companies bring in outside caterers to the office for important, large-scale lunch meetings. For lunch meetings, alcohol, in moderation, is acceptable. Business dinners tend to take place in restaurants rather than at home. Cocktails after work are commonplace.

Office hours:

Business hours are officially Monday to Friday 0900-1730, although an extended working day is very common in certain sectors and it is not unusual for people to be working well into the night or over the weekend.

Economy:

The US economy is the world's largest, most technologically powerful and diverse. Distinct benefits arise from a unique combination of mass immigration, technological and marketing innovations, vast natural resources, expansion of international trade, historical fortune and an economic system designed to reinforce professional and personal enterprise.

The enormous influence of US-based multinational companies within the world economy affords unparalleled global influence and allows its currency unique international status.

Large areas of the USA, particularly in the Midwest, are under cultivation and produce a wide range of commodities; important are cotton, grain and tobacco, all exported on a large scale. Principal mining operations produce oil, gas, coal, copper, iron, uranium and silver. US industry leads in steel production, automotive manufacturing, aerospace technology, telecommunications, chemical engineering, electronics, computer-based commerce and manufactured goods.

The largest employment is in the service sector, finance, leisure and tourism. If for no other reason than its role in the world economy, the USA is an important conference destination; there are state, city and regional travel and convention organisations in every part of the country, each actively promoting its own assets. Three of the largest convention and trade show venues in the USA are Las Vegas, New York and Chicago, with Las Vegas holding the top position for a number of years.

Good Luck!